KARIN JARMAN was born in 1953 in Baden-Baden, Germany. She studied Waldorf Pedagogy at the Goetheanum, Switzerland, after which she settled in Great Britain where she worked in a Camphill centre for adults with special needs. In 1985, together with her husband and three children, she moved to Gloucestershire and studied Art Therapy. From 1990 she worked as an art therapist at St Luke's Medical Centre in Stroud. Karin helped establish the Hibernia College of Art Therapy, and has run courses both in this country and abroad. She is currently facilitating spiritual support groups for people with chronic health issues and life crises via the organization she established called Oasis.

TOUCHING THE HORIZON

*A woman's pilgrimage across Europe
to the castle by the Golden City*

Karin Jarman

TEMPLE LODGE

Temple Lodge Publishing
Hillside House, The Square
Forest Row, RH18 5ES

www.templelodge.com

Published by Temple Lodge 2008

A catalogue record for this book is available from the British Library

ISBN 978 1902636 94 8

Cover by Andrew Morgan featuring a photograph by Pavel Bednar
Typeset by DP Photosetting, Neath, West Glamorgan
Printed and bound by Cromwell Press Limited, Trowbridge, Wiltshire

This book is dedicated to my maternal grandmother, Elsa. When I was a little girl she told my mother to take good care of me because I was a special child. Fortunately my mother told me this only much later when I was already grown up. But I wish that every child in the world could have such a grandmother, who believes in a child's uniqueness. This gift bestows an inner strength and a sense of security, as well as trust in destiny whatever it brings.

My grandmother told me fairy tales, because she loved me. There was never a time in my life when I did not believe in the truths contained in these stories. Even later in life, images from fairy-tales have been an inspiration for me whenever I had to make difficult decisions, and in my encounters with other people.

And in my 49th year, it was the power of these images that led me to undertake this pilgrimage.

Contents

Photo Credits:

Photos of Karlstein on pages 14–15 of plate section © Pavel Bednar.

Photos of the inside of Karlstein on page 16 of plate section © Management of Karlstejn Castle.

The Publishers would like to take this opportunity to thank sincerely both Pavel Bednar and the National Institute for the Protection and Conservation of Monuments and Sites of the Czech Republic for their generous permission to allow reproduction of their photos of Karlstein in this publication.

Acknowledgements

Writing this book following my pilgrimage has been a journey in its own right. I remember the day during my pilgrimage when I pledged to write this book as a means of thanking all the people I had met and who have helped me on the way. Upon my return to 'daily life' it seemed a mammoth task to fit this into my busy art therapy practice, having to learn computer skills almost from scratch. Seven years after completing my journey the book has now emerged with the help of many special people.

The editor of *New View* magazine, Tom Raines, asked me to write an ongoing description of my pilgrimage *en route*, and so helped me to rediscover my love of writing, out of which the idea of a book naturally followed. My publisher, Sevak Gulbekian, encouraged me to submit my book for publishing; an idea which had never occurred to me. I thank him for waiting so patiently all these years! I would like to thank Zambodhi Schlossmacher for typing the German version in order to enable me to work on the English. Both these pieces of writing would have been stuck in the computer forever had I not had the most generous sponsorship from two very special friends, Joanna and Tony Wilson, who made it possible to produce a manuscript with the help of a professional editor. Aonghus Gordon provided sponsorship to have my paintings included in the book, for which I am deeply grateful, also for his words of support for my inner journey right from the very beginning. Further financial contributions have come from Debbie Leek, one of my early hosts.

The book itself is my heartfelt *thank you* for all the generosity of people who have given food and shelter to the pilgrim on her way, without which the journey could not have happened in the first place. And even before that, I need to give special thanks to my close colleague Marah Evans who had a deep understanding of my impulse to touch the further horizons, and for letting me go! A group of friends from Camphill and Trigonos Centre blessed my journey some months prior to starting with a special supper, the spirit of which stayed with me throughout. My wonderful three children, Hazel, Odilia and Melvin, accompanied me inwardly with their love and encouragement. Finally, it was Bernard, my life's companion, best friend and husband, who knew in his heart that my time had come to be parted from him, and who never wavered in his trust that this open-ended journey would eventually take me back again to him, even though I could not have known this myself. This, more than anything, is the most precious gift and sign of being truly loved and understood.

Karin Jarman
Stroud, March 2008

A Note on the Colour Plates

I have often been asked whether I did paintings and sketches whilst on my pilgrimage, or whether I took photographs. Regarding the latter, I had made a conscious decision not to take a camera with me; somehow this did not fit with my image of a pilgrimage, which is much more about inner process than admiring the landscape. As far as painting is concerned, I did actually take with me a small watercolour travel set, which I used to paint postcards to send home or to my students at Hibernia College, who were following my journey by sticking pins into maps. Apart from my week long stay in Belgium with one of my hosts who had a painting studio, I did not do any serious artwork until I returned home. And then I had first to overcome the huge blockage which I describe at the end of this book.

After a while I was able to create a meditative mood out of which I could paint with the three colours, indigo, magenta and gold. The images that presented themselves to me through these colours became the relics of the Karlstein Castle, which, after all, is where the inspiration came to build the castle in the first place. They became like small 'prayer images' which connected me with the practise of deepened meditation with which the emperor Charles IV approached these relics.

The inspiration for the sequence of pastel paintings on the Foundation Stone Meditation came to me after I had learned the verses off by heart during my journey through Belgium,

and while I stayed with my host who had the painting studio.
I made some sketches there to explore my initial ideas, which
I then later turned into these paintings.

The most human part of the human being is the foot. Hands are dedicated to the human soul. The feet however seek a direct connection with the earth. They extend our spiritual nature.

Dr Bruno Callegaro, 26 January 2001, Kassel

*

The suction-like characteristic of light becomes manifest in the life of the soul. The light would like to draw us out into wide expanses. Our gaze is in constant danger of losing itself in the distance. The gaze wakens in us a longing to actually step through, measure and experience the space which the light opens up.

Dr Paul von der Heide, *Spiritual Therapy*

*

Harbouring spirit gift within
is my intuiting sense's strict command—
that ripening endowments of the Gods
in soul depths forming fruit
bear fruits to my selfhood.

Rudolf Steiner, *Calendar of the Soul*, verse for the week of 21–27 July

Beginnings

There is gold at the end of the rainbow. We only have to find out how to get there.

As a child I loved to gaze into the distance. Each time I did so it awoke in me the longing to reach the horizon. Later, when I was a bit older and could reach a far-off point, another horizon appeared before me! And so again I had to set out and discover what lay beyond.

Thus was born my love of walking, which to this day continues unabated and as strong as ever.

Like many others I have always been drawn to the elusive nature of *the end of the rainbow* and its hidden treasure. And yet somehow I still believe that one day I will be able to reach it. That is why I can never give up my questing, longing, or walking. I have to thank my grandmother for this conviction, for it was she who enchanted me with the wonder-filled world of fairy tales. I have always been able, even in the worst and darkest hours of my life, to find great comfort and strength in the wisdom of these tales—which speak of how, in the end, we can attain even the remotest and most highly prized goal, though of course this can never be a simple matter. A sacrifice will always be necessary. One might have to cut off one's little finger to make a key, or perhaps promise never to laugh or cry for a full seven years. I remember when my father told me the story of the enchanted swans and of their sister who, to free them from a magic spell, was not allowed to laugh or cry for seven years. Then he looked at me and said: 'You wouldn't manage that would you?' He chuckled and I thought to myself, 'No that sounds far too difficult. But if it had to be ...' So far I have not been put to the test on that one!

Fairy tales also tell how the traveller must be friendly towards all whom he meets on the way—unassuming or even ugly beings, perhaps a wise old woman or even giants or dwarves. They could also be ants or bees, eagles, wolves or foxes... Whoever they are, each one must be shown due respect. By this means the traveller finds the helpers with precisely the qualities he will need to fulfil the difficult tasks that lie ahead. It may also happen that the traveller falls asleep at a crucial moment and misses the most important thing, and then has to start again from the beginning. Or, while returning home after having already reached his goal, he may be robbed of his prize. He must then find new courage to reveal his true identity when the right moment comes.

The truth is that after overcoming innumerable obstacles on the way, the traveller will, in the end, always achieve his goal.

As a child I always wanted to go somewhere—to go travelling—these words had an almost magical effect on me. Indeed my earliest memory is of being found by my worried father after having run away at the age of two-and-a-half. I was standing at a crossroads, and the moment I was found I knew that I had done something that I should not have done. Before that moment I was blissfully unaware!

I have enjoyed walking ever since, whenever the opportunity has arisen. If I have to think about something, work through an inner problem or need new inspiration, I go on a walk. I never return disappointed.

During the course of time I discovered inner horizons, and found that they were not dissimilar to the external ones: a journey through the inner landscape was accompanied by many surprises, happiness, sorrow and obstacles. And again the longing arose to discover what lay beyond the next horizon.

Luckily I came across people who were familiar with these landscapes. I remember for example meeting an old, white-haired man when I was $18\frac{1}{2}$. He had worked as a night watchman for a great many years and had come to know the night sky almost better than he did the earth. From him I learnt to look upwards into the heights. I needed this so as not to lose myself in the darkness down below. The starry skies gave me comfort during times of darkness. Since then I also enjoy walking at night.

Later on I became aware that walking not only involves moving forwards, but also that an ever-increasing distance extends behind us as we journey. This became a new riddle for me, and an inner experience of the transforming power of journeying. Walking on foot is the most ancient form of travel. In many cultures it is a form of ritual. At the turn of the millennium I had the chance to spend a short time walking with Bedouin people and was able to experience their deep relationship to the earth. I have always been fascinated by the medieval tales of travellers, pilgrims, bards and journeymen. These are colourful stories full of adventure and surprises. The story of Parzival and the inner quest for the Grail continues to have a special meaning for me.

When I was in my thirties I met a genuine pilgrim. This person made a huge impression on me. He travelled on foot, had virtually no baggage and his shoes were worn through.

He stayed in our house; and our children, who were quite young at the time, couldn't leave him alone and were continually asking him questions. He came from India and described how in his homeland it was a tradition for everyone to undertake a major pilgrimage once in their life during their fiftieth year, in order to take stock and gain new perspectives on life. His name is Satish Kumar and he is the editor of *Resurgence* magazine. This encounter made a powerful impression on me.

I became aware during the course of my own journey that it is also important to the earth for us to connect our rhythm with hers. Through our feet we learn love for the earth, and how she bears us and provides the foundation for all that we meet in life. I firmly believe that the earth can sense our love and find some relief through it from everything else with which we burden her. Nature awaits our perceptiveness, and to develop this it is important not to go too fast. The astonishing truth is that the greatest distances can be covered by developing the patience simply to place one foot after the other. Time and space begin to take on quite different dimensions—and herein lies the greatest mystery and wonder.

So it was that a longing grew in me to undertake, once in my life, a journey that would not bring me back to my starting point but rather bear me ever further into the blue distance. I have often gazed at the wonderful turquoise colour of the sky on a summer evening and sensed how it would like to draw me away from my body and lead me out into the infinite. There lies the new, the unknown, the realm of the possible. I wished to open myself to new experiences and new meetings! When would be the right moment to do this?

I had often thought of walking the Silk Road. Pictures of

those different cultures spoke to me very strongly, the names of exotic places sounding as if from a fairy tale: Samarkand, Uzbekistan, Turkmenistan, the Gobi Desert, and many other magical places. People of other races, strange and wonderful architecture, bare earth and new horizons beckoned me. I knew, however, that as a woman on my own I could not manage it.

Then I considered the old pilgrim route to Santiago de Compostella in Spain; but since today it is so well trodden, I soon abandoned the idea. I also felt that it would be important for me to formulate my own destination. It would not have to be a recognized place of pilgrimage but somehow be connected with my own life's journey.

In the summer of 1999 I experienced the sun's eclipse in Cornwall. I felt the disappearance of the sun's light as a deep inner pain unlike any I had experienced before. It was several days and nights before I came fully to myself again. The event strengthened my resolve to learn to distinguish between significant and insignificant things. For this I needed time, rhythm and loneliness, and a distance from the demands of daily life.

Shortly after this experience I woke up one morning with a very clear picture in my mind of the Karlstein Castle in Bohemia. Immediately I knew that this was to be my journey's destination. A long trek from the south of England to Bohemia was something I could realistically consider; after all I would be able to make myself understood during most of my journey.

I felt a particular connection to this castle. Some three years previously I had visited it with my husband. At the time however we had been unable to go to its three sacred chapels, which are counted amongst the most precious treasures ever to have come from the spirit of Central Europe.

Wenceslas and Karl IV

The Emperor Karl IV built the castle in the fourteenth century to house the crown jewels and priceless Christian relics. It was never intended as a fortress, but to represent a threefold image of human existence: worldly responsibility, religious devotion and the free human spirit. The innermost room became the emperor's place of meditation, a place where he could find direct communion with the world of spirit. The castle lies at the centre of Bohemia, above the Beroun river valley. It is not far from Prague, which Karl IV made his glorious capital, and which, at the very heart of Europe, was for a long time the centre for alchemists, Rosicrucians, artists and social reformers.

Though historically well documented, the figure of the much-loved Karl IV is clothed in many legends. Even today the Czechs express wonder and reverence for this remarkable person.

Karl IV for his part felt a deep connection to St Wenceslas, an ancestor of his and the patron saint of the Czech people. St Wenceslas had been taught and, one may assume, also initiated into Christian mysteries, by his grandmother Ludmilla. He was later murdered by his brother at the doorway to a church as he entered. Karl IV had a chapel built in his honour within the great St Veits Cathedral in Prague. Its walls, like the chapel in the Karlstein, are decorated with gold and inlaid with semi-precious stones. There are also frescoes and inscriptions from the holy texts and the life of Wenceslas. In addition to this, the Emperor recast the ancient crown of the Premyslid dynasty, from whom both Wenceslas and his own mother descended, and created the so-called crown of King Wenceslas. From then on this was used at the coronation of Bohemian kings.

As King of Bohemia St Wenceslas gave considerable support to the Order of the Knights Templar and permitted them to build their own church in the city of Prague.

Karl IV was christened Wenceslas. It was only later at his Confirmation that he received the name Karl. His father was from the Luxembourg Royal Family but throughout his life Karl felt inwardly more connected to his mother. This explains how he came to feel the deep love for Bohemia which came to expression on his accession to the throne and also later when he was appointed Holy Roman Emperor. As a child he formed an enduring connection to Wenceslas, his ancestral forerunner, spending hours writing out the legends connected with him, and seeking to emulate him in whatever way he could. Later, as the King of Bohemia and as Emperor, he developed Prague into a prestigious city. The social and administrative structures he created were far ahead of their time—which is perhaps why they did not survive beyond his lifetime. Karl IV founded the University of Prague and, by making Czech its language of study, made it accessible to his people.

We can see therefore how Karl's gaze pointed in two directions: partly back to the past via a deep connection to his maternal ancestry, and partly to the future and the new Age of Enlightenment which signalled the end of the Middle Ages. Another polarity can be seen between his inner devotional life of meditation, divine service and contemplation, and his worldly cosmopolitan activity which drew artists and scientists from all over Europe and helped Prague to blossom.

Bohemia—imagined and real

So what is the link with my own biography? This showed itself at first in some very small and apparently insignificant soul experiences of my childhood. My storytelling grandmother once gave me a dolls' tea set made of porcelain. Each piece was inlaid with a rim of gold. I think she had noticed how much I loved to see her bring out her own special set of china and glass crockery which she told me came from Bohemia. Bohemia? That must be a fairy-tale kingdom, such as those she described to me in her stories: roads paved with precious stones, a landscape of hills, dark woods and castles filled with mystery. I connected the image of deep red, transparent glass and precious gold with the name Bohemia—an image of a profound transforming passion that lies hidden deep within the soul, awaiting the moment when it can be brought to consciousness.

There is also a nursery rhyme, 'Pommerland is burning...' In my childish mind, Pommerland was not far from Bohemia. It was destroyed by flames, but as a result Bohemia was spared. I held an inner picture of this imagined landscape and was therefore amazed to discover, when I came to journey through it, how closely these images corresponded to reality. Its hills looked as though they had been made by children in a sand pit. Each was unique and appeared individually crafted.

I am only able to give a pictorial description of this deep

inner relationship. Later I learned in a more conscious way that Prague is a highly interesting cultural crossroads at the heart of Europe, a place where East, West, North and South encounter one another. This is visible in the art, architecture and philosophy that has blossomed there. Prague is also one of the few cities where the Jewish people could feel secure and welcome during their medieval persecution. This can be traced back to an old legend in which the Libusa, founder of both the city of Prague and the Premyslid dynasty, had a dream in which she foresaw how fleeing refugees without a homeland would arrive in the future; and that they should be taken in and warmly welcomed since they would help to enrich the town and bring it further wealth and fame.

The geography of the Czech country—her waterways flowing in three different directions, to the North Sea, to the Baltic and to the Black Sea—also shows it to be a crossing point of different streams.

I discovered those motifs again in my own biography. My ancestors originated from the centre of Germany, the very heart of this country, part of which became Communist Germany after World War II. This caused my parents to move west to start a new life, and this is where I grew up with my brothers and sisters, in a small town between the Black Forest and the vast plane of the Rhine. I myself moved even further west later on, to Great Britain, where I started my own family. I immersed myself deeply in the Mysteries of Celtic Christianity, which defied the influence of the Roman Church and formed communities based on brotherhood rather than church hierarchy—in fact, very similar to the ideals of Karl IV. It was interesting for me to find out that the Celtic people had also inhabited Bohemia before the Premyslids settled there.

The whole destiny of Central Europe since the two World Wars is deeply moving. The Iron Curtain all but obliterated the intrinsic mediating quality of that culture. For over two generations it brutally divided the heart of Europe through differing ideologies and political systems, causing a deep rift between the generations growing up on either side of the divide. But for some people these events became the catalyst for a heightened awareness of the deeper meaning of the mission of Central Europe over and above ideology, religion and economy. The citizens of the city of Prague, for example, have shown amazing courage and ingenuity in upholding basic human rights and dignity in the face of political persecution, even fighting to the death for what they believed in.

I began to see my pilgrimage in this light. In all humility it could be a small contribution to rebuilding a bridge across this divide. It was something which I, as a single human being, could do: measure the distance with my feet between Europe's West and East.

These thoughts were not what ultimately moved me to undertake this journey, however. They belonged to my day consciousness and helped illuminate the impulse that came from a much more hidden depth of my soul. I see the origin of my decision in those images of my childhood that I described at the beginning of this chapter. The ruby red colour of stained glass, deeply loved by me since childhood, became the symbol of my pilgrimage.

Stepping Out

For a whole year the impulse to undertake this journey lives in me. At first I only speak about it to the people closest to me—my husband and children and my closest colleague. I know that a lot will depend on their responses. With my husband I discuss the fact that we have reached a turning point in our relationship as our children are now adults and the youngest will soon be leaving home too. Afterwards a lot will depend on how we can find each other again. Our connection needs to be renewed or come to an end. This is a turning point that needs to be acknowledged.

My husband meets me in this space, courageously. He will indeed let me go, without knowing whether I will return to him or not. This is the most precious gift I have received from him.

Many conversations with my children and my colleagues follow, and I feel that I receive their blessing and understanding. I am very fortunate indeed.

However, this is not true of everyone. My parents are aghast at hearing about my plans and find them irresponsible. One or two friends voice similar concerns. I need to listen carefully to these voices as well. I, too, wrestle with doubt. Why indeed do I want to do this? Isn't it after all a mad idea to just leave everything and go?

I pace up and down and can't find any peace. I am plagued by heavy dreams. I find it difficult to hold a coherent train of thought. I have many conversations with people but they come to nothing...

I have bought myself walking boots, but they don't fit properly, they hurt and chafe ... and they cost me a lot of money. Then I buy my backpack. I look in the mirror to see what I look like with a backpack on. Cursed vanity! I am supposed to think of other things now, so many things, and I'm sure I've forgotten the most important ones! Where will I sleep at night? I do have a few addresses, but they are mainly in England. Once I have crossed the Channel I've no idea where I'll stay. And what about my children? Will you forget me when I am gone? I will not see you for such a long time! My friends, my husband! With what kind of thoughts will you accompany my journey? I will be a *stranger*, a terrible word: it means one doesn't belong, one is cast out. Will I be able to bear it? I have experienced what it means before in my life; when I was 17, and without a home for three long years. I may be homeless again now on some occasions, who knows? Why do it? I have got my house, my hearth, my bed, why should I leave it all? I have my profession which I love; I have colleagues who value my work; I can be creative, paint, write stories; I can cook interesting meals, make my house beautiful; I can visit friends.

I have got everything I could possibly want, I don't need anything else. I am happy with myself, exactly as I am; I have learned that, practised it, and I teach it to other people. Every day I do my meditative exercises as best I can, even when everyday matters constantly intervene. I will learn to curb my vanity, to be gentle and considerate, to be there for everyone selflessly; I could study more, could carry on learning to become ever better at my work as a therapist. I may even still turn out to be a real artist after all; I have only to find more time to practise, learn to be patient. Patience! Yes, this is my downfall, I am not known to be patient! What would I give for this virtue! Perseverance, yes, that is not a problem for me; I am tenacious (some say obstinate). What else do they say about me? Do I really feel happy as a German citizen in England? This is something people always draw attention to: 'Yes, you're German; that's why . . .' Am I not surrounded by prejudice? Isn't it time to do something about that? After all, I am already at the end of my forties, people expect me to have achieved something by now. Who am I? Where am I? What have I actually achieved?

Where is my love and my warmth? Is it still needed in the world, the little I have? The inner turmoil spills into the night. During this time my dreams are of pregnancy and motherhood. A little child is entrusted to my care. It is completely dependent on me. I have to nurse it, but then it slips away from me and goes its own way. I find myself alone. I meet the king's son who had been promised to me but he no longer knows me. Again I find myself alone.

What fruit can be born of this loneliness? With whom will I be able to share my thoughts? In the Bible story, Tobit sends his son to the marketplace to find himself a companion for his journey,[1] but I have to go by myself and perhaps no one will be with me. I actually don't have to go, I could decide to stay after all, I could call off the journey and pretend that everything can carry on as usual. I could do that. I would have to somehow explain this to myself, but it could be done.

My inner world is in turmoil. People ask me how I feel now, whether I am getting excited. What, they ask, are you hoping to get out of your journey? Will you be different when you return? I ask myself, what will become of me? Will I meet other people's expectations? What are my own expectations?

Actually, I do not have any. There is no way I can know how it will all turn out; I have to be open to the new thing that wants to happen. That is how it will have to be. I have to determine both the outer and inner aims myself as I go along. Even now I know that it will be the path and not the goal that will bring about transformation.

Yes, I do want to change. But into what I do not know. I don't want to know it either. It's got to show itself to me; it cannot be predetermined.

But now I realize that I am not sufficiently prepared for this journey, neither outwardly nor inwardly. I am scared and I have to face my fear.

On one of these days of doubt I am walking with my daughter through the snow-covered landscape, spreading before us as though enchanted. The stream is edged with ice flowers, and the hills seem newly sculpted; the beech woods emanate their profound silence. Christmas Day has passed and there is peace on the earth. Can my heart be open to its message? So close to my departure, I cherish the company of my eldest daughter. On New Year's Eve we are with friends. During these Holy Nights a great deal is happening within me. On this night we prepare the biodynamic 'Three Kings' Preparation',[2] made from the substances which the Three Kings brought as gifts to honour the Christ child's birth. Small portions of gold, frankincense and myrrh are ground up at midnight using a pestle and mortar. This 'dynamizing' process is done on New Year's Eve. On Three Kings' Day the semi-fluid substance will be stirred rhythmically in water and sprayed over the land as a healing medicine and blessing for the earth.

On completing this task we do some lead-casting for fortune telling.[3] Each one of us is given a difficult message; in my case it has to do with facing up to a few ugly bits inside myself. But we are really pleased! For myself I know it to be very appropriate as I am still wrestling with my anxiety and fear, and negative thoughts about the pending journey, as well as my shame about the untransformed parts of my soul. So the difficult message is all too visible to me and I rejoice! I am getting so much help from my friends!

A few days later I wake up out of the following dream. I am a man and a soldier going to war. There is a huge battle and imminent danger of death. I have to hide in order not to be killed. My enemy is getting ever closer. I put myself flat on the ground and my head and upper body change into part of the nature around me; I allow it to happen. The enemy is looking for me and steps on that part of me that is now nature. I try to control my breathing, with difficulty; he will discover my trick at any moment! But no, he gives up the pursuit and pours water onto that place. I am glad that he is not wanting to light a fire.

The following night, that of my birthday, I have another dream. I am travelling by train, with many other people. I am busy with my thoughts and find it difficult to talk to the other people, even those I know. The stations we pass and the trains are grimy with dirt, impersonal. I don't feel well in these surroundings. Then I realize that I am waiting on the wrong platform, and with a lot of effort I finally find the right one, only to see the train disappear in front of me! I have to wait a long time for the next train and this wait turns out to be futile.

My journey is to begin the next day.

I am about to enter the age-old community of pilgrims and I am reflecting on what it means to be a pilgrim. In the first chapter of her book, *Sacred Journeys*,[4] Jennifer Westwood speaks of pilgrims and the pilgrimage:

> What is it that they seek? Why in all ages and all over the world have people felt the same desire to set out, launch themselves as it were from a springboard out of their normal lives and familiar places on a journey into the unknown? The answer seems to be that, to whatever faith they belong, wherever their footsteps are directed, and whichever immediate reasons they give for going, at bottom all pilgrimages spring from an inborn yearning for an encounter with the divine.

For one thing you have to travel on foot, I think, even though I have heard of pilgrimages on horseback or with a donkey that carried the luggage. But I imagine the true pilgrim on foot. He has to travel in poverty. The person who inspired my journey, Satish Kumar, even stipulated that one should travel without any money at all. I did think about that but in the end decided against it, because to start with I am not from India where they still have a functioning culture of hospitality. I did, however, read the story of an Englishman who also knew of Satish Kumar's advice and who actually managed to walk the distance from Plymouth to Edinburgh without any money at all—a remarkable achievement![5] But then I am not a man, and the thought of being completely at the mercy of other people's help for sleeping arrangements did not make me feel comfortable. It might not always be offered selflessly. I have to make my own personal risk assessment, like anyone has to when they embark on their own undertaking or journey.

I don't think that a pilgrimage has to be undertaken in a religious context. I would say that a journey becomes a pilgrimage when you are as much on an inner as an outer journey, seeking a dialogue between the two, and this becomes the central meditation. Without this willingness to explore the inner world, there is no pilgrimage.

I have mentioned already that for me personally it has been very important to decide my own destination and to travel by myself. Of course there are pilgrimages where several people journey together, otherwise we would not have the wonderful *Canterbury Tales*, in the course of which the pilgrims provided entertainment for each other, told sad and funny and also lewd and rude tales that are utterly delightful! Yet I had a great longing to be by myself. I love my fellow human beings so much that I would be entirely distracted. I would not be able to enter into deep communication with the earth, the landscape and nature, which for me is the essence of journeying. It engenders such a deep resonance within me that I can only compare to the ecstasy of lovemaking. After only a few miles I find myself deeply immersed in an experience of intimacy that reaches down to the core of my being and becomes the presence of what is around me; I become one with it. When I return it is as if I have woken from a deep, regenerative sleep.

That is why I can never think of pilgrimages as ascetic and as punishment for some sin. Pilgrimage means life in its fecundity, means loving, savouring, reaching into the fountains of creativity, and can contain within all that the deepest pain of truly meeting one's own being. It means a conscious severance from the matters of daily life, and requires inner effort to let go of dearly beloved habits for the duration of the journey. It does mean work and one has to be prepared for renunciation and discomfort, but the reward is such that those words do not feature in my consciousness.

Thus pilgrimage is not penance, as I see it. It is certain that it will change you, perhaps beyond recognition. No one who undertakes a true pilgrimage will return as the same person that he was before. It is impossible. Just *how* this change will manifest itself needs to remain open. I find it important not to form any preconceived images: you may find that the change is completely different from what you imagined and even hoped for, or what others expected it to be! A journey full of such expectations is bound to end in disappointment.

Part of the preparation involves consulting the people with whom one is closely connected. I was fortunate that my husband, children and closest colleagues at work showed an immediate, intuitive understanding of my longing to go on a pilgrimage. I know that without their blessing I could not have accomplished it. Then, in the course of time, these people were joined by others who accompanied me with true interest, joy and even admiration. Many have told me that my example has given them courage to listen to their own inner voices and do something they had not dared to do. In this way I felt myself surrounded by a kind of mantle woven of the thoughts of many people.

Poverty, chastity and obedience were part of the culture of the monks and nuns of medieval times. I needed to rediscover the meaning of those words for myself as a modern pilgrim.

It was my intention to travel with as little money as possible. In our time it is actually a great relief to be freed from the unnecessary burden of consumerism for a time, and to realize that it is possible to manage without it. I don't think that it would have felt like a pilgrimage if I had taken money along in the same way as when going on holidays. I therefore became a lot more dependent on other people, which in itself was a great lesson to learn.

I discovered chastity in the way I could meet other people as a pilgrim. It is quite an amazing experience to find completely new possibilities of meeting with people who at first may not even have a concept of contemporary pilgrimage. Many people were deeply moved by their encounter with this possibility of 'walking the talk'. And I endeavoured to open myself completely and purely, with clarity and purpose and without desire. That is chastity.

Obedience belongs to freedom! That was the most surprising discovery. It is no longer possible today to impose tradition and outer rules on a pilgrimage, even though it may still be practised like that in an ecclesiastical context. The decision to undertake the journey can only arise within oneself. Once the decision has been taken, the challenge is to remain obedient to it, not to give in to the inner and outer voices of doubt. Before anyone else knows of the decision it would be easy to postpone it, to put it to one side or even forget about it. Only your resolve to remain faithful to what you have experienced in what may have been a very short moment, to remain faithful to the spark that led to your decision, will help you through. This continues even after you have already started out, as even then you may lose sight of this precious moment for a time and be plagued by doubt and rational voices that wish to persuade you of the futility of your undertaking. The temptation to cut the journey short may arise at times of particular hardship. Only the sacred obedience to your innermost resolve will help you through this desert. Obedience enables you to come to a free decision anew at any given point, though this may sound like a paradox!

On the eve of my departure I have a huge birthday party and the house is filled with friends. What can you give the pilgrim who has to carry everything? I am amazed at the ingenuity of my friends. I am given poems specially written for the occasion, foot balm, socks, lightweight torches, a four-leaf clover, flowers, tiny precious stones, runes of blessing and a little travelling icon. This icon really did accompany me all the way to the Karlstein, marking my sleeping place every single night! I placed it, along with a night-light, by the side of my bed and thus it graced all the stations of my way.

One of my friends who comes to the party, Rosemary, is terminally ill. For five long years she has been battling cancer, which has disfigured her once beautiful features. She has fought with astonishing courage and still is fighting, and I ask myself whether I will meet her again when I return. Our gaze meets for a long time. I cannot believe my ears when finally she says, 'You are a courageous woman!' Me? Courageous? I have certainly not thought of it like that. Under no circum-stances could I compare my courage with hers in her battle with illness. I say this to her. She too is on a journey. Oh, I know of some of her agonies, of some of her restless search for healing, of trying and failing with a number of miracle cures. Yet throughout she never stopped living. Still she searched and wanted to live, but not to go back; she was truly a pilgrim.

All our journeys will end with an encounter with death, and most of the time we live unaware of this. Sometimes it needs a diagnosis, or the sudden death of someone close to us to bring this truth home to us. We are repelled, we do not wish to face it. We cling to what we think we have. What can we really take with us across this threshold? What of our love, what of our hate will travel with us, perhaps without us choosing it? What will we put into our luggage for this journey? Will there be someone to receive us, to help us find our orientation in a new and strange country? I realize that my journey is a tiny little rehearsal for this big one. In Rosemary's presence I can feel it strongly. Maybe this is why so many pilgrimages, including mine, are to places of holy relics—bones of people who lived long ago.

Many well-loved things I will have to leave behind that normally would be extremely important to me. Also, I will have to be parted from my loved ones, from people whose company I gladly cherish every day. I will have to face the unknown, never knowing where I will arrive. I have chosen to be on my own. Our last and final journey can also only be taken alone. There is a very narrow passage at the end that does not allow for even two people to squeeze through. But once this passage has been crossed there is absolutely no turning back, and that is the big difference from my journey. If necessary I could always decide to turn back. So, my friend Rosemary, you have the greater courage by far.

I look into her eyes for a long time. I know she is already a long way into her travels. There is joy and gladness in her eyes, perhaps even something of the joker. We embrace, there is not much left of her. Then she presents her gift; it is a freshwater pearl necklace. 'This is a free gift! If you would like to pass it on to someone else on your journey, you may do so!'

Now it is really hard to take my leave. And yet I can hardly wait till tomorrow. I am in a dream; I can no longer really join in with the party. It feels as if I have become transparent. It is painful and I retreat into the dream. It is comforting to have so many friends here and yet I deeply long for solitude. It is a truly sacred moment.

Surprisingly, I sleep very well. My backpack is ready—and heavy enough, even though it only contains necessary items. I know that my biggest challenge at first will be to carry it. It is a beautiful and sunny winter's day, and Three Kings' Day too. Today the precious preparation we made on New Year's Eve will be sprayed upon the land, as medicine; only I can't be part of that. Instead, I will lovingly walk over the earth.

I have breakfast with my husband—I cannot describe my feelings during this, our last meal together. In myself there is a melting pot of emotions, expectation, impatience, pain, but no longer any fear. I am ready now; there is joy in my heart, now I must go! These first footpaths near my house are well known to me. I make steady progress and climb the first hill. Then I look over my shoulder for a last glimpse of my house, the street and all the familiar sights, and tears stream down my face. This is not because I am upset or sad. This experience will repeat itself many times during this journey; at this point, though, it is totally new to me. It is as if the soul is completely overwhelmed and needs to respond somehow. Or, put differently, that I am overwhelmed by my own being.

A little while later I meet up with my godchild and her parents. She and her father wish to come with me on horseback to Cirencester, my first stop for the night. Here the landscape of the Cotswolds opens up to our view.

Soon I can't keep pace any more with my friends. My backpack is too heavy and my feet hurt. Kelvin carries my rucksack for me for the last stretch. If only I could do without my backpack, it would be pure joy!

At lunchtime we reach Cirencester Park. Some time ago, on

one of my local walks, I somehow found myself locked in this same park, behind the high walls after dark, and could only get out again by cunningly waiting until one of the residents opened the gate. So this time I was mightily glad to see the church spire of Cirencester town in daylight and in a direct line with my footpath! After our picnic my friends take their leave and now it is all up to me! I know all the footpaths around here and my first hosts are good friends of ours, so I am not out in the wild yet. They are expecting me with a warm bath and a lovely meal. I notice huge blisters on both my feet.

On the following day I know: *This is it.* Now I am on my way, journeying. I settle into a new rhythm. At first I am very much aware of my body; my limbs are aching and my feet are suffering badly. By three o'clock I feel worn out. All my concentration is fixed upon the footpath signs so as not to lose my way (as has already happened). There is not much time or energy to focus on my inner landscape or to get into a meditative mood. And yet I am already lost to the world as I have known it. Already I find myself unable to identify with my former self, and when I think about it I am astonished by how quickly this has happened. When I arrive somewhere in the evening and my hosts ask me about my life and occupation, I speak about my former life as if talking about someone else altogether, with warmth and even enthusiasm but without identification—because I am here now, and *here* represents my entire life!

As I walk I increasingly experience the distance I have covered. Already I am in unfamiliar places. And now I can see with my own eyes what previously I only learned from reading the papers: the terrible after-effects of the severe flooding that had ravaged England the previous autumn. My days are still bathed in this wonderful wintry sunlight, but the land around the rivers and streams is muddy and makes walking extremely difficult. Often my feet sink into the mud as far as my shins and in the effort of pulling them out again, my shoes rub against my blisters. Every step hurts like hell. Sometimes I think of turning back. Often I find my path blocked by water and I have to make a huge detour—by now I have encountered a few footpath signs that pointed straight into a lake!

The earth is suffering and I suffer with her. She bears my pain. This helps me to identify with the far bigger pain the earth endures. Is this why I had to make this journey; was this the only way to make me see what is really happening with the earth? It is so easy to forget this in everyday life unless you are affected by it directly; now I can feel her pain with every step I take. The earth sheds her tears too. Why did I not see this before? I also see the beauty that lives in the destruction wrought by the floods, in the glittering water everywhere that mirrors the blue sky of these beautiful, frosty winter days.

It is around lunchtime of the fourth day that I reach Wayland's Smithy. The mighty structure of ancient pre-historic culture speaks a strong language. I hear the wind playing melodies in the bare winter trees as I shelter amongst them; it is cold, freezing cold. Now I walk on the ancient Ridge Way that has seen traffic for thousands of years, and I think of all the millions of travellers whom this road has carried. It is badly rutted by the past rains and the wheels of modern vehicles that have forced their way onto this track without considering the consequences. I see signs everywhere asking horses and vehicles not to take this route. I can see fresh traces of motor bikes. Walking becomes ever more tiresome, if not nearly impossible, and I have to continuously negotiate between the middle of the path, the deep ruts and the numerous puddles. A lonely man and his dog come with me for a little while. His wife has left him; he has only his dog. He loves the old Ridge Way and often comes walking here but he has never seen it in such a bad state. As we reach a summit I can see a long stretch of the way still ahead of me, which I will have to cover by this evening. He wishes me luck. 'It is still far,' he says, 'and already the light is failing.'

My painful feet have fused with the pain of the earth. The throbbing can no longer be ignored. I weep, but they are different tears from those of the first day. Welcome to the pain! Already I am able to really say that. Welcome.

Totally spent I arrive at my hosts in Burbage near Marlborough. They give me a footbath. The next day they take me to a doctor's surgery; the blisters on my left foot have become infected. I have to take an antibiotic and have a day of rest. The medicine makes me very sleepy...

I continue with raw, sore feet along the Reading Canal now with the icy east wind blowing directly into my face. It is really hard going. I am aware of the military barracks that I am passing now, flanked by barbed wire and thorny thicket— with this on one side and the canal on the other I feel trapped.

At one point I take off my socks and shoes to examine my wounds. I become aware of a man jogging along and after a while returning again. For the first time I feel fear. Why did he come back again so soon? If he really has evil intentions there is nowhere to hide and nowhere to flee to. Quickly I chase these thoughts away, but I know that I much prefer to walk over open fields, meadows and woodland rather than these canal paths. I can admire the ingenuity of their construction, built during the Industrial Revolution, and see that they have a beauty of their own. But I am also aware that they force the water to flow in a straight line and the surrounding landscape is altered accordingly, whereas rivers are inherent features of the landscape itself.

But there is one advantage to walking along canals—you can't get lost. It is like the motorway; you get straight to the goal. And because I don't really have to navigate much either, I find that I can concentrate my thoughts on what happens inside me. Except that I am rather focused on the pain in my feet just now! Stoically I continue, but need to pause frequently. At the end of the day my strength is utterly spent; I couldn't walk another step.

My blisters are so bad that they arouse the deepest compassion in my lady host. The thought of turning round and going back again visits me quite often now. I have to admit that I have overestimated my stamina, and perhaps there is a greater strength in admitting defeat. Nobody will hold it against me, I am sure. However, the next morning I feel strength and courage returning, even though the pain of my feet is as great as ever. I decide to continue and to bear the pain, and once again I dive into the rhythm of walking that sustains me. Finally I reach the wide-open countryside again, which receives me and gives me great joy and I can forget about my weariness.

England

I don't know why I love the English landscape so passion-
ately, nor can I explain it even to myself. I have to reach back
into my childhood again. England was a magic word for me,
though in a different way to 'Bohemia'. I had of course no
real concept of either of them. 'England' continued as a theme
when we learned English at school. I remember the intense joy
of my first English lesson, and running home to my mother
afterwards declaring that now, at last, I was able to speak
English! I also loved my English teacher to bits.

Having lived in England for more than half my life, the
country has become my home. I love it here. I love the way the
trees grow in the meadows, standing like strong individua-
lities, each with a character of their own. I love the bleak hills
that appear like massive sculptures, sometimes further
enhanced by huge images of horses or giants drawn into the
chalk, or by stone circles, dry-stone walls and hedgerows. The
ancient people of this land must have felt the need to explore
the interior secrets of some of these hills and built inner
chambers or tumuli into which, to this day, you can creep to
listen to the dark and the silence.

Yet the beauty of the landscape alone is not sufficient to
explain my strange connection with England. Often when out
walking I feel a very distant memory rising up within myself,
and just at the point when it might reach the surface of
waking consciousness it disappears again. A tender and yet
aching sensation is all that remains. What is the message that

is trying to reach me? It may come again, only to be lost once more. It comes in waves and goes again. I try to catch up with it with my feet and never reach it. The search continues to this day, and the ensuing restlessness contributes to my need to walk.

The first three weeks of my pilgrimage take me through parts of England that I had known previously only when driving past on the motorway. Then I had not been able to distinguish any particularly attractive features. How different an experience it is to walk through the same landscapes! It is pure joy! When I finally leave the canal path I continue onwards to the south of London, avoiding the city. From time to time I have to cross a motorway. I recognize this aspect of 'my former life', the everyday reality dictated by speed and efficiency. I look down from the motorway bridge onto the constant stream of traffic, then turn my back and gratefully enter the stillness of the woodland. It is an important reminder that one day I shall have to return to this kind of life again. Will it feel different then? Will I ever be able to travel at such speed again?

The motorway crossings become more frequent the closer I get to Gatwick Airport. Here I can see how greatly the landscape has been affected by development. When the morning mists that have lain like a veil of enchantment over the fields begin to lift, I can see that the earth has been poisoned—it shows in the plants and the trees. Nature no longer provides protection here, but is in need of it herself. Now, in the harsh light of the midday sun, I see the wounds inflicted on the earth and realize that it would not take much to turn the whole area into a concrete desert.

After leaving this part of the country behind I come into

the ancient county of Kent. Here I experience again the aftermath of last autumn's flooding. The ground is saturated with water. Despite this I am again captivated by the beauty of the countryside, which is now very different in character, with its red brick houses and their mighty ornate chimneys, each with a different pattern. From my hosts I learn that this particular area was the home of the architect Sir Edwin Lutyens (1869–1944), who connected himself deeply with the old English tradition of house design and endeavoured to revive it.

I have to make many detours here. My original plan of walking along the river Medway has to be abandoned when I sink almost knee-deep into the mud. Instead I head for the heights and find another route into Maidstone. Here I decide to take another day of rest.

When I visit the city the next morning I feel like someone from another planet. I have to buy a few simple provisions, and find myself almost incapable of choosing from the vast array of merchandise. With great relief I continue walking the following day. In the meantime my feet have completely healed; I can walk in a steady rhythm instead of stumbling along, and I am in high spirits. I want to move on!

The new day brings a very special gift that has stayed with me ever since. I am now walking the North Downs Way, which is an ancient pilgrims' route in part—the one to Canterbury. The path runs along the ridge that borders the wide plane leading to the coast. A few days previously I had visited St Martha's Hill near Albury, and the special little chapel there. Now the path leaves the woodland for a while and I can gaze out into a vast distance with the blue hills folding into each other and stretching back as far as the eye can see in the clear winter sunlight. A deep recognition rises up within me that my long held desire to walk into the blue distance is now being fulfilled! For the first time I experience this distance not only ahead of me but also behind me and I can say: I have walked everything I can see! And I recognize the depth of longing that I could not have ignored without peril. I am utterly filled with a sense of gratitude that my destiny has brought me to that inner place, and this feeling continues to accompany me now for the rest of the journey and beyond.

This day, which opened an inner sanctuary, echoes and reverberates, and brings to birth a further dimension. The mystery of time and space open up in an immediate, experiential understanding as I realize that I have come from an infinite distance on many life journeys and that a further infinite distance still lies ahead of me. The fact that I have covered a certain part of that distance with my feet has brought about a profound change in me. I realize that *space* does not remain indifferent to the deeds that we do in *time*, and that, through our human actions, we transform unformed potential into earthly reality.

I believe that this sacred moment brought me closer to the secrets of birth, destiny and death: I was able to grasp in one brief moment the meaning of our existence on earth. It was much, much deeper than simply understanding it. It was there and was gone again almost in the same breath, but the memory of it has stayed with me and still fires me with enthusiasm whenever I call it up. And for me it is not without significance that this experience happened in England.

My destination for tonight is a very interesting village by the name of Wye, which even boasts a university. This is what I learn from my host who is very proud of this fact. He is an architect and lives, with his teenage son, in a huge house that he has built himself. From there I continue on a dull day, with a raw east wind, over hills and valleys to the ancient pilgrim destination of Canterbury. I have to struggle through the dreary suburbs until I reach the famous cathedral, which I approach with inner expectation. I am taken aback by the fact that you have to pay admission charges to enter the place! I feel indignant that church has become business; Christ expelled the merchants from the temple after all! However, on announcing that I am on a pilgrimage I am allowed in free. But I am not so profoundly touched by the splendour of the interior, comparing it unfavourably with my beloved Gloucester Cathedral. Then I discover the pilgrims' hospital nearby and am grateful that people have thought of that, too. During the evening of this day the sky fills with indigo coloured clouds. There is moisture in the air.

Two days after this I am again on the North Downs Way and the last stretch to the coast lies ahead. I can feel the change of direction as the path now curves southwards and the sea gets ever closer. I have one more station on the way, in Barfreston with its particularly beautiful Romanesque church and also a community house of the L'Arche organization.[6] I don't meet anyone at all in the village. Everyone, I think, is sitting by their open fires, away from the cold and damp of late winter outside. But I have to face it the next day, relentlessly, as I fight my way through the ubiquitous mud in constant drizzle. But that does not diminish my joy on reaching Dover in the late afternoon—I have accomplished the first leg of the journey! Tomorrow I shall leave England and step onto new territory. The Channel is a true border; from now on everything will be different.

Hospitality

Before I cross the Channel I have to acknowledge my hosts and say a little bit about them. Hospitality used to be a sacred duty. In our culture this has changed drastically. Children grow up knowing they have to be wary of strangers. Danger lurks everywhere and increases the more that outward security increases. The human psyche remains unpredictable. How can you explain that a 'nice' neighbour turns out to be a monster who secretly abuses little children? Or that the seemingly wholesome family next door harbours destructive relationships? And why does everyone tell me that it is dangerous to walk by myself as a woman?

It is completely understandable that we tend not to open our doors to complete strangers any more today, whereas in former times it would have been impossible to go travelling without the sacred duty and tradition of hospitality. In bygone days there would always have been an extra space by the hearth; a bit more water would be added to the soup and a spare corner would be found for sleeping when the traveller knocked on the door, without interrupting daily life too much. The traveller might even be regarded as the bearer of special blessings—like Christ, who was thought to walk unrecognized among people and sometimes ask for hospitality. Perhaps he would reveal himself at the moment of leaving or be known by certain signs and miracles after his departure. Also, people were aware of the biblical saying: What you do to the humblest of my brothers, you do unto me.

That's how it was in the past. Today it is understood, at least in the western world, that when you go travelling you take enough money with you to pay for board and lodging, or else refrain from travelling altogether. Instead of the open door and a welcome, the door is more likely to be double-locked. This is no doubt prudent, but our culture is the poorer for it.

I remember one day when a stranger knocked on my door. It was totally unexpected. At that time we lived in an old seventeenth-century cottage in a little village right by a busy main road. When I opened the door it might as well have been the seventeenth-century! In front of me stood an old man with a long beard full of tiny icicles, dressed in rags, with a large sack slung over his shoulders. He told me that he was hungry, and could I give him a piece of bread? I asked him in and made some hot breakfast that he devoured with obvious relish, after which he asked for a second helping. Meanwhile the little icicles had formed a puddle around his feet; his cheeks had turned a ruddy red and his features relaxed into a wonderful childlike expression. Only after he had left did I remember that it was 6 December, the day of St Nicholas!

Now I am just such a tramp myself! I am filled with the feeling that I am homeless. I don't find it easy, at the best of times, to ask for help, to make myself dependent on other people. I tend to forget, along with most other people, that it is an illusion to think that we can be independent of our fellow human beings, even and perhaps particularly so in our present time. And I also forget, along with nearly everybody else, that every human being who crosses my path is really a unique revelation!

My very first hosts on this journey were Virginia and John. We knew each other from a few visits and when they heard about my idea they immediately offered their hospitality. John is a true English gentleman and his wife is from Ecuador, with the temperament and warmth of heart to go with it. Immediately on arrival I was greeted with a warm and luxurious bath and beautifully soft towels. Virginia remembered my favourite dish and had also invited some friends for me to meet. John took a great deal of trouble pulling out maps and explaining some footpaths to me that he knows from his own hiking.

My second host was Deborah; again someone whom I had known before, and both her bathroom and the delicious dinner have stayed in my memory! Deborah, too, had invited a friend of hers to the meal, who took a great interest in my undertaking.

Many of my subsequent hosts I found through having joined a hospitality organization called Servas. On hearing about my plans a friend of mine had told me of Servas which was started, shortly after World War II, by a group of Quakers. Their idea was to enable people to meet one another in a spirit of hospitality, to work towards mutual understanding and friendship across borders. Today Servas is a worldwide organization. After an initial interview members are given address lists of people who make their homes available to travellers, free of charge. Each member follows a 'code of ethics' so that hosts are not taken advantage of, and travellers feel safe and protected. I must have stayed with over a hundred Servas hosts along the way and found them all to be special people with a great diversity of lifestyles and philosophies.

My first Servas hosts were Liz and Adam who lived on a farm tucked away in the village of Coleshill. That particular day had been extremely hard work for me as I had struggled through the mud and puddles. I arrived in a state of utter exhaustion, covered in dirt. Adam cheerfully introduced me to the hosepipe that he uses to clean his gumboots. He is a young farmer, full of enthusiasm and conviction. His equally cheerful wife greeted me in her huge kitchen, by the Aga, and despite my aching muscles I was urged to look around their rambling farmhouse right away, so that I would feel at home. Their bathroom was as big as my living room at home! It turned into a jolly evening, with their two daughters Rowan and Laurie and a visiting friend from the States. I felt truly at home and resolved to keep contact with this family upon my return. Liz walked with me about a third of the way the following morning. It was one of those sunny clear days on the early part of the walk, and there had been a frost overnight. We were both deeply touched by the beauty of the countryside leading up to the Ridge Way.

My next hosts, who had to deal with my sore feet, were Diane and Roy in Burbage. These people had written to me in response to a small announcement which I placed in *Resurgence* magazine, and invited me to their beautiful thatched cottage near Marlborough. Here I had my first day of rest to visit a doctor's surgery. Roy and Diane looked after me beautifully.

Other hosts I had been put in contact with through friends who had asked them on my behalf and who had been glad to meet me and look after me. Sometimes, when I had no accommodation the following night, someone might ring a friend some 20 kilometres away, and in this way I found somewhere to stay every single night whilst walking through Britain.

Everywhere I met with real interest and human warmth, food and lodging being given freely, not to mention the baths and showers that I so looked forward to. Very often there were deep conversations and real human encounters. I met them in the midst of their daily lives, yet they created a space within that to meet a stranger and make a small, festive event. Nearly everywhere we celebrated somehow!

On the seventh day of my journey an interesting incident took place. I had just left the Reading Canal and happened to be passing the Alderbridge Steiner-Waldorf School. As my own children had attended a Waldorf School I felt interested enough to visit this one. The building was surrounded by a high fence and I went through the gate into the yard. It was break time and a few children and adults were about. I found a bench and proceeded to eat my packed lunch and watch what was going on. But one of the teachers quickly approached me and asked me in a very friendly way to leave, as strangers weren't allowed to enter the school property. I understood immediately. Schools are under enormous pressure from health and safety regulations, and since there have been nasty and even fatal incidents on school properties both in the USA and in this country it was only prudent to protect children from strangers.

Nowadays it is really no longer wise to trust strangers, at least where children are concerned. But this means they have to grow up in a world of suspicion and be surrounded by security measures. They can watch all sorts of adventures taking place on screen but they themselves are mostly denied such experiences. There is no longer much opportunity to be a young hero.

After I explained myself to the teacher, however, I was

cordially invited in to take part, for a little while, in the games lesson and to tell the children about my journey. So I left with joy in my heart about this special encounter.

That same evening I reached Mortimer and realized with amazement the total change in the landscape. It is a gently undulating area with boggy ground, pine trees and heather. For long stretches there are no proper villages, but single farmsteads in the few valleys. It is quite a different mood here, more pragmatic, with greater width of space and a feeling of loneliness. The roads cut across it in straight lines and in the end I had to resort to road walking; there were no more footpaths. I thought it would never come to an end.

That night I stayed with Ruth and Meir and I met Ruth at my arrival carrying bags of shopping into the house. She is an older lady but was full of youthful energy as she busied herself in the kitchen, talking to me all the while. Her husband is an artist who creates large wood sculptures, which I was invited to view in the garden. They also had another guest that night, Gloria, who came to have a quiet weekend with Ruth and Meir. This was a Jewish household and as it was a Friday the evening was dedicated to the Sabbath celebration. A blessing was spoken that permeated the whole night and continued to accompany me a little on my path. They invited me to spend the following day with them and took me on an outing to see an old Roman camp nearby, Silchester, which the Romans called Caleva. We took a walk around the earthwork and afterwards visited the very special chapel nearby, a strange and beautiful spot imbued with a feeling of solitude and peace; it seemed as if this generous open landscape could happily accommodate the ancient Roman and the later Christian site next to each other in complete harmony.

That Sunday I continued my walk with gratefulness in my heart. This kind couple seemed to me like old Philomena and Baucis, lovingly entwined and glad to welcome guests into their dwelling whilst being full of stories of their own extended family. By lunchtime I found an open barn; I was glad of the shelter and took out the packed lunch that Ruth had prepared for me. It had been lovingly put together, a nourishing cheese and ham sandwich, complete with some raw carrots so that I had something fresh, too, and a bar of chocolate as a treat for afters. How much this meant to me! Silently I send my thanksgiving to Ruth, together with my blessing—now that I am a pilgrim I can give blessings, too!

With my next host family I experienced the positive effect on children of a culture of hospitality. As I knocked on the door, it was opened by their 16-year-old son who immediately took my bag from my back; the 9-year-old ran into the kitchen to put the kettle on, and the youngest, aged 5 perhaps, entertained me by showing me his toys. Later I found out that he, the youngest one, had offered his bedroom for me so that I could have my own room and he would camp down with his brothers. These children were evidently used to welcoming strangers straight into their family and to making them feel welcome. They could meet the world with openness and trust.

My onward journey took me via an old pilgrims' route to Albury (near Guildford). It was already pitch black before I arrived at Linnea and Roger's house. They are practising Buddhists and were expecting friends that same evening for a common meditation. I was invited to take part, too, and to speak about my journey. Here, also, I was urged to take a rest day and I found, finally, that my feet had healed up completely and I felt sure they would not give me any further trouble.

Then there was the household of a bachelor that lingered in my memory for quite some time. Peter lived on his own in a fairly spacious house, which he only spent time in after work, to eat and sleep. He spent a long time that evening speaking to his girlfriend on the phone, explaining to me that they did not have a lot of time to see each other and that they really needed to change things in their lives to be able to have time for their relationship. Right now he was buried in work, and so was she.

A few days later I called in on friends, Bons and Tijno, in Maidstone, who had written to me before the start of my journey and invited me to come. Bons, in particular, had been looking forward to my visit, as she had walked part of the Camino de Santiago in Spain, so we sat together that night and compared notes. She also insisted that I took her tele-scopic walking stick, and I subsequently found many occa-sions when I was truly grateful to her for this. Many a time, I'm sure, it saved me from serious injury.

Yet another episode of hospitality comes from my stay in Wye, with Patrick and his teenage son. I sensed a profound sadness around Patrick despite his sunny and joyful disposi-tion. He had lost his beloved wife, and mother of his son, to cancer. I sensed her presence in virtually all the corners of the house, and in my bedroom there was a wardrobe still filled with her clothes. Several photos showed her striking features and petite frame, and with a gaze soft yet full of determina-tion. Patrick told me about her and his grief at breakfast time; he opened his heart to me and talked of his inner agony and deep depression. His wife had been his anchor in life. Now he had to somehow make do without her for the sake of his son, and try to be a good father to him. It was difficult for him to continue living in the house they had built together, which was full of memories of her. He wanted to leave and make a new start somewhere else and find healing and peace.

I found it hard to take leave after this conversation—how could I leave this man behind in his sorrow? I carried a layer of sadness with me. I longed to meet Patrick again to continue our conversation.

People will open their hearts to a pilgrim. After all, he will leave again and take the stories along. The world is full of such stories. Often on my nightly walks in the past I looked at people's houses from the outside and tried to get a glimpse of the inside through the lit windows, pondering on the destinies of those living there. This journey now gave me plenty of opportunity to look into other people's houses, to briefly touch into their destinies, only to continue on my way again. All these encounters are engraved in my heart, have shaped it and changed it. Often I wonder how these stories continued.

To a certain extent this happened with my next host, Melanie, whom I had briefly met before in the context of my work. We are the same age, but Melanie will never be able to go on a pilgrimage on foot. Five years previously she became paralysed as a result of a life-saving operation, and from then on her life changed drastically. Her thoughts and deeds have become purposeful and self-directed in a way that had not been the case prior to her illness. She resolved to dedicate the rest of her life to the service of others, particularly those who struggle with illness, bereavement and loss, wishing to bring to them her own experience of the search for meaning and spiritual significance. Melanie expressed a wish to work together with me upon my return—I am deeply touched, only I don't know how I can possibly find the same kind of courage that she shows.[7]

Water

Water often marks a boundary. For example, the English Channel has always been one. Even today when the British talk about Europe they do not include themselves in it, because you always have to cross the water somehow if you want to leave Britain. Now I have to wait five hours for my ferry, so it is already late at night when I finally arrive in Belgium, at Ostend. Luckily my host has offered to pick me up and take me back again in the morning so that my footpath is not interrupted.

But where is the footpath? It appears there is no such thing in this part of Belgium. Nobody travels on foot here. Every inch of the earth seems to be covered either by buildings, roads, monotonous parkland, factories, shops and the like, or it is highly cultivated, endless fields. If you don't want to travel by car, you ride a bike. I am taken aback. Where is the European long-distance footpath? I just can't believe that I will have to walk along roads, but there is nothing for it, not a single footpath in sight. Then I find that you can't even buy walking maps, only bicycle route-maps.

I wish I were somewhere else. How will I be able to put up with this for the three weeks it might take to get through Belgium? I am filled with longing for England. Then I make a quick decision to leave the road (which is marked as the long-distance footpath) and follow the canal instead. The path along it is also tarmac but at least it's away from heavy traffic and noise, and only now and then does a car come by. Now that I have left the way-marked route, I orientate myself around this country's elaborate canal system. You can be sure that the canal paths will invariably lead you somewhere. Most of Belgium's canals are still in use; indeed, often you find that they follow the main roads too, but at least from time to time they reach into the more open landscape, particularly the further east you go.

Today I am surrounded on all sides by water, also from above. In fact, it is absolutely pouring with rain—an unremitting grey sheet of water that penetrates absolutely everything, so I am left soaked to the skin. I ponder the straightness of the roads, the canals, the rain mixed with the greyness—this is my first impression of Belgium. It must feel like punishment to live here, I say to myself. Everything seems so dreary and tedious; pragmatism rules, leaving no room for beauty.

Then my thoughts extend further, to how the water is so like the unconscious part of our soul and how one can also drown in that. Particularly if there is no light. Water without light lets you go under and lose your centre. Perhaps it is for this reason that people have always tried to tame water, to force it into straight channels so that it can be subservient to our needs. But in the same way that our subconscious will not allow the conscious mind to rule it completely, so the water will also fight back at some stage. Water needs a different type of understanding, but on a day like this it simply becomes too much for me and I long to escape it. Since I can't, I retreat into my inner world.

A few days later, however, I have a wholly different experience with this element. I am now in the medieval city of Brugge, enjoying the glistening sunlight playing on the water of the canals that criss-cross the city. It is still surrounded by the old city wall, shaped like a giant egg and edged by yet another canal. Most of the houses are at least 300 years old, and some of them still show the splendour of a bygone age.

I find out that Brugge is a city connected to the legend of the Holy Grail. In its cathedral is a relic said to contain a sample of the blood of Christ, and each year on Ascension Day this relic is displayed and paraded through the town in a festive procession. Blood is the human equivalent of water; it flows through our body like the rivers that penetrate the land, and is born and renewed deep inside the firmest part of our body, in the bone marrow. The blood is also like a sense organ for our whole body in that it conveys messages from one part of us to another. Historically, the merchants, travellers and those seeking adventure have carried messages and been carried by the water, bringing different cultures into contact.

I now have a long distance to cover on the border of the waterways, and it is here that my outer path transforms itself into an enduring meditation. After a while I am carried along, freed from the need to navigate as the water continually guides me. I resolve to learn something by heart that I have wanted to learn for a long time and never found the opportunity. It is the Foundation Stone Meditation by Rudolf Steiner, which will accompany me daily from now on.[8]

After some time I am able to discover the more hidden beauty of this country as well. I enjoy the constant mirroring of the sky and the clouds on the water surfaces. The open stretches of fields with their hedges and bare winter trees remind me of Flemish painters of the sixteenth to seventeenth centuries.

It felt very special to approach the three cities of Brugge, Ghent and Antwerp on foot like a medieval traveller, walking from one to the next. They are like precious gems strung on the necklace of the waterways. Ghent is a proud city indeed, with high turreted towers and splendid buildings full of elaborate decoration. I spend a long time with the famous altar of Ghent, painted by van Dyke, and admire the clarity of the colours in blue, green and red, and the lovingly painted, minutely detailed nature studies that give me an impression of how the Belgian countryside might look in the summertime.

My route into Antwerp is along the river Schelde. What a relief it is to follow a natural river bed, which winds and meanders. The early morning mist leaves its veil over the river banks and transports me into a different world. Now I have to cross the river, and I find out that there are still real ferrymen here who dwell in wooden huts: you have to knock on their door and ask whether they might take you across! And they promptly do so, even if you are the only passenger, as I was; and they don't take any money for it. I pass an island in the river with a multitude of birds and I see a painting in my mind's eye of blues and greys and white; and I take a deep breath of the fresh and clean air, before tackling the vast suburbs of Antwerp.

Antwerp harbour is bigger than the city itself. I can feel the great openness of this place, communicating with the world, being open to other influences. The city has a large flourishing Jewish community that has historically con-tributed to its wealth. I discover an underground passage below the river that connects one part of the city with another. There seems to be constant movement; people here are on the go.

My first host in Antwerp is a jolly bachelor who produces a wonderful dinner and then lets me have free run of his house as he has to go out that night. I love its colourful atmosphere, with velvet curtains, paintings and sculptures, big indoor plants and a fluffy cat. I curl up on the sofa and feel at home!

I Need Help

The following day I spend with Rika who had read about my journey in a magazine and invited me to stay with her. She is a delicate and reserved person and it is difficult to get a conversation going at first. This made me feel quite insecure and uncertain how to approach her. But it did not take long for Rika to show her warmth and friendship, together with her partner Ider. She shared a lot of her personal history with me and told me quite a bit about her friend Mia with whom I am going to stay next.

Mia lives in a village called Zeursel. To get there, I initially follow the Albert canal, which is the biggest in the country and flows right through the middle of Belgium. It is a very wide canal to accommodate the many vessels that travel its waters. Further to the east of Antwerp I finally chance upon real footpaths again, leading me through some lovely woodland. Finally I reach the fairy tale house of Mia, who lives here with her adult son. There is a welcoming open fire burning in the living room as the weather has turned very cold again. Wonderful smells waft in from the kitchen, and soon a four-course meal is brought to the table. Mia has so many stories. She is an older person with white hair, who looks deeply into your eyes. She reminds me of the Mother Holle of the fairy tale. At first I am a little overwhelmed, just like in the story, and then I find such a good and generous soul who longs deeply for human company. We discover that we have much in common. I don't find it easy to take leave the following morning. My Frau Holle tells me: 'Remember, if you need any help at all, let me know!'

That night is the first one without an actual host, in an old people's home: Mia had telephoned ahead for me, and asked them to put me up. From there I continue along the Albert Canal again.

Great clouds gather in the sky as I walk by the water. Suddenly the clouds part and piercing sunlight streams through the gap like a spotlight. Part of the landscape is lit up by it, bordered by deep dark shadows, and on the opposite bank there are the glistening red rooftops of a village. Again I am reminded of the Flemish painters, and have to admit to myself that this flat stretch of landscape has its own beauty and magic, and served as an inspiration for painters through many centuries. I can now see why: the great expanse of sky with its ever-changing drama, and the water that constantly responds to those changes; the gnarled willow trees; the houses that promise comfort and shelter, whatever the weather brings. The sky above me is like a painting in its own right, so I no longer miss the variety below as I am captivated by this play of light and shadow.

Two days later I am very ill. I have no strength at all. I am continuously sick and can't keep anything down. I am housed in a spare room full of junk, which is part of a special needs community, and the staff cannot look after yet another person. I remember Mia's words as we said goodbye. I phone her, and half an hour later she arrives to pick me up. So it happens that I spend quite a few days in Mother Holle's house. Outside the snow begins to fall, to complete the picture. I close my eyes and allow myself to drift into oblivion; the world around me dissolves and every now and then Mia's voice drifts into my consciousness. It feels so good to be looked after and not to have to worry myself about anything at all! If this had happened before my encounter with Mia I would have felt utterly helpless.

Five more days I spend with Mia and her son Phillipe, and she nurses me back to health. I am given wonderful food and soon I can take a stroll through the woods with her; we watch a bright red sun through the thicket of trees like a precious, medieval stained glass window.

I do a lot of reading and also some painting. Some text by one Jesaiah Ben-Aharon catches my eye:

> ... to stimulate and encourage people to find the way to inner freedom and independence. To this end we need to bring together individuality with community and celebrate our encounters with presence of mind and a living humanity, whatever form it may need to take to bring it to expression ... I am interested in people who wish to bring a spiritual quality out of their own experience into everyday life ...

I find these words very inspiring and formulate the wish to see each and every encounter as an experiment in creating something wholly new between me and others. I want to learn to find the uniqueness in each human being and to rejoice in that which is new, fresh and possibly unrecognized if it defies the patterns of our normal expectations. This is a way to experience the spiritual world in the here and now.

Outside the snow continues to fall. After my flu I am plagued by toothache, and I begin to think that I might have to abandon my journey for the time being. Mia finds a dentist who is willing to treat me and I am filled with a kind of dread prior to my appointment. It could be serious. The dentist might tell me I need extensive treatment, in which case I would have to return home. What would such a verdict feel like?

I have to wait for my appointment over the weekend. That night I have a very strange dream. I encounter a beast covered in a stinking ugly slime and tethered in a cage. I know that this being is not evil, that in its core it is a good being although I am utterly repulsed by it. I also know that I have to free it from its cage. This is made difficult by the fact that there are malevolent beings lurking in the background who will try to overpower me. I need all my will-power to overcome nausea and fear, and I have to proceed very quietly indeed. On waking I recognize that this dream is connected with a correspondence with my father who greatly disapproved of my journey, accusing me of selfishness, arrogance and pride. At the same time, though, he urged me to visit him and my mother whilst in Germany, even though their home is 300 km off my route. I can feel that something is approaching me that could have big repercussions for the rest of my life, something big and powerful, which I need to meet with the utmost presence of mind. For now I have to let the matter rest and make my decision at a later date, seeing as I have to leave everything open at this stage. I only found later that this dream was indeed a prophetic one.

On Sunday Mia suggests an outing to Lier and I look around this splendid little town with some fine examples of the Flemish tradition of the Bejinhof houses, a kind of early example of social housing—quite unlike the infamous workhouses in England. They were originally inhabited by women who had decided to live a celibate life but did not want to become nuns. This was not, at first, accepted by medieval society and they needed special permission from the pope (Gregory IX) to be allowed to carry out their social work. I had already seen some examples of Bejinhof houses in Brugge and, as with the ones in Lier, was impressed by the beautiful atmosphere around them. Here they were, still partly inhabited and therefore even more impressive with their lovingly tended front gardens. Lier also boasts a most unusual clock tower, named the Zimmer's Tower after its inventor. It contains an astronomical clock with incredibly intricate mechanisms that show the time everywhere in the world, as well as the movements of the stars.

Monday is the day when the decision will have to be made. I spend the morning painting in Mia's big studio and in the afternoon Mia presents me with a very special surprise. She takes me to a place called Tangerlo, to an abbey where you can see a perfect replica of Leonardo's *Last Supper* fresco, painted by the school of Leonardo and surprisingly similar both in content and quality to the one in Milan. The abbot himself shows us round—even though the abbey is normally closed to visitors for the winter—and tells us the history of this astonishing work of art and how it came to be here. He had heard about my pilgrimage and wanted to meet me—Mia couldn't have thought of a nicer surprise for me! The abbot tells us that part of the building is used as a hostel for pilgrims on their way to Santiago de Compostella from Holland. I listen very intently—perhaps it might be possible to approach some monasteries and ask for hospitality as well!

I brace myself for the dentist's appointment. He prescribes some medicine; again I have to resort to an antibiotic and he advises me to have extensive treatment in three to four months' time. But at least he gives the go-ahead to continue on my journey for the time being if I respond to the medication. That tells me that I mustn't drag my feet, yet must also be ready to listen to my body and if necessary change my plans.

But for now I can continue! I enjoy my last night in the soft bed in Mother Holle's house, and then I am ready again to face the uncertainties of my pilgrim's way of life.

I remember that I do not have an address for the following night. I decide not to mention this to Mia, she has done so much for me already and I don't want to feel too dependent on her ever-willing help.

A Small Interlude

For today I am homeless! Mia takes me back to the Albert Canal, we take fond leave of each other, and then I steel myself for the journey ahead. I go with a heavy heart. I am unhappy about having to take the antibiotics. And I feel increasingly uneasy about not knowing where I will sleep tonight.

My path continues along the canal, endlessly, and I am passing the most bizarre industrial landscapes of towers, pipes, tunnels and chimneys belching foul-smelling smoke.

On studying my map I find an abbey marked on it some kilometres ahead, a bit further than I would normally like to walk in a day. It is the abbey of Merkenrode, and remembering the words of the abbot I think to myself that I might as well knock on their door and ask, assuming they would probably think it very unchristian to turn me away. I drag myself along the last two kilometres at the end of a long day, but also with great anticipation. When I ask my way in the village I am directed beyond it again, through boggy ground with wooden planks that I can hardly see in the failing light. But I can see some lit windows and make out a road in the distance. Then I reach the abbey and my heart misses a beat: in front of me is a ruin and building site with notices not to enter, and no human being in sight whatsoever! The lights that I had seen belong to some outlying farm buildings and there is no one who can help me. I am utterly exhausted and hungry.

I sit down and proceed to tell myself off for this foolishness as I have no one else I can scold for it. I am very hard on myself indeed: what a stupid idea it was all along! I remembered that I had met a very nice woman in the village when I asked for directions and she would surely have helped me out, but now it was too late; everybody will have gone inside and all the shops are closed—and I am so utterly exhausted.

After some searching I find a pub full of people and I ask someone behind the counter whether they might have a bed for the night. They mention a price which sounds pretty steep, but I nevertheless follow the landlady upstairs to view the room. It is untidy and dirty and the woman is grumpy, not at all pleased at the prospect of having to get a room ready for me. I decline. Someone in the pub whispers to me that this was a wise decision on my part.

That night I have no choice but to sleep in a hotel.

Only much later, in the French-speaking part of Belgium, is my wish to stay in a monastery fulfilled. I am a guest in the Abbey St Rennache Wavremont. I approach it on a misty evening through ice and snow and a deserted wilderness of ancient woodland full of bog holes—a landscape that speaks the language of my heart after the dreariness of the canal walks. And I am received with great warmth and friendliness even though none of the monks speak any English and I don't speak any French. I bathe in the atmosphere of devotion and am deeply touched by it. During vespers I find tears streaming down my cheeks and I realize that I have not heard music for so long. My soul is longing to linger here.

In the vast plains of Flanders I don't have to concentrate on signposts as I simply follow the canals. Of course, there can also be all kinds of obstacles. The path can suddenly turn into a major road or it might simply stop altogether; and I always have to be very aware of which side of the water to be on as it could be several miles before the next bridge. But most of the time I am faced with long stretches of paths unrolling ahead of me towards my next destination. I just have to watch out for the many cyclists in their garishly coloured outfits, like giant insects, whizzing by.

As mentioned earlier, whilst walking along I take the opportunity to learn the Foundation Stone Meditation by heart, which Rudolf Steiner gave at the founding of the Anthroposophical Society at Christmas 1923.[8] Even though this meditation is connected to this very specific event, one can experience its universal relevance for our time. I had tried to live with this meditation many years before but had not found it easy to penetrate, even though its structure fascinated me. I knew I would have to learn it by heart to immerse myself in it fully. Now, without the demands of daily life, I find my opportunity.

I start reading it and then learning the lines, supported by the rhythm of my walking, and listen while certain lines and verses speak to me:

Human Soul!
You live in the limbs

I am living in the limbs as I walk and cover the distances of my path! I feel my limbs as they carry me and give me the foundation of my being. Since this is what I am actually doing, I can feel its relevance right through my bones.

Which bear you through the world of space
Within the flowing ocean of the spirit:

This, too, I experience daily now since the mystery of space opens up to me as I walk through it. Space envelops me and lets me go again as I move on; I am forever in this alternation, as new space receives me again. I feel a deep gratefulness to my limbs which so faithfully carry me through the breadths of space, serving me selflessly.

Practise *spirit re-cognition*
In depths of soul,
Where in the wielding will
Of world creating
The individual I
Comes to being
In the I of God;
And you will truly *live*
In your body's cosmic being.

This remembrance of our divine origin, of the divine spark that has begotten us and given us the solid ground of the world in which to experience our own being, is what carries and sustains us. It is original Love itself, capable of creating life, making existence possible. By incorporating this mood into our daily life, a deep feeling of gratitude can arise.

For the Father Spirit of the heights is present
In world depths begetting existence:

This is how it was since our beginnings, and still is. It sounds from above and is received below.

Human Soul!
You live in the beat of heart and lung

I step from the mystery of space into the mystery of time as I cross space by the strength of my limbs alone, which completely alters my experience of time.

The next part of this stanza speaks about being present in the moment and I realize that this is still a huge challenge for me, that I am still often caught up in the past or projecting into the future.

> Practise *spirit presence*
> In soul composure,
> Where the weaving deeds
> Of universal becoming
> Unite
> The individual I
> With the I of the World;
> And you will truly *feel*
> In the active life of your soul.

It takes me a long time to learn this particular part by heart. I am fascinated by the beautiful crafting of this stanza and can visualize it to myself as a mighty movement of colour.

> For the Christ Will is present all around
> In world rhythms shedding grace on our souls;

These lines were an inspiration to me even before starting out. In fact, I can trace the impulse to walk into the distance to an experience of the circumference of the earth, of being held in its embrace. Often, when dusk fell, I looked out into the clear, blue distance above the light of the setting sun and felt drawn longingly to the horizon.

> Spirits of Light!
> May what is formed by the west
> Have been quickened in the light of the east;

And here I am on my journey, going forever east!

Proclaiming:
In Christ death becomes life.

The feeling that arises from this part of the meditation is COURAGE.

Human Soul!
You live in the stillness of the head
Which from the founts of eternity
Discloses for you cosmic thoughts:
Practise *spirit beholding*
In thought calm,
Where the eternal aims of Gods
Give the light of spirit worlds
To the individual I
For will in freedom.
And you will truly *think*
In the founts of your human spirit.

These lines seem to arise as if out of an icon painting where the colours in their golden splendour have come to rest and have taken on a timeless feel. A sacred and celebratory mood pervades the following lines:

For the Spirit's cosmic thoughts are present
In world existence begging for light;
Spirits of Soul!
May there ascend from the depths
The plea heard in the heights;

These words are so beautiful and deep. It is possible to gain the gift of freedom through the will of the Creator-being. The reverse movement to the first stanza takes place, bringing a mood of prayer in which we can move towards future possibilities of development, at the same time gaining strength and trust in destiny, to endure even the difficult parts of our lives.

The meditation closes with a single verse about the birth of the Christ-being into earthly conditions. It helps to bring a more human dimension into the mighty images of the other verses:

At the turning of time
Cosmic Spirit Light descended
Into the earthly stream of being;
Darkness of night
Had run its course;
The light of day
Shone forth in human souls:
Light
That gives warmth
To poor shepherds' hearts,
Light
That enlightens
The wise heads of kings.

God-given light,
Christ Sun
Give warmth
To our hearts;
Give light
To our heads;
That what we found

From our hearts
What we guide
From our heads
Will be good.

I now live every day of my pilgrimage with this meditation, and I feel the strength and courage I gain from it. Later in my journey I take to reciting it in the silent and remote woodlands of eastern Germany—after making sure that no one else is around. Then I feel how nature itself receives and responds to those words...

In the meantime news reaches me of the foot-and-mouth epidemic in England. On my hosts' television screens I watch in horror the slaughter and subsequent funeral pyres of vast heaps of animal bodies, reminiscent of the Holocaust. It is strictly forbidden to go out walking in the countryside—if I had set off only two or three weeks later I would have been unable to walk through England.

I hear of heartbreaking stories of farmers who cannot bring themselves to let their healthy animals be senselessly killed but are forced to do so in the end. They are told that this is a necessary preventive measure if the farm is within a certain radius of an infected one. Here in Belgium and later on in Germany people speak of England as if it is a country of lepers, where diseases break out at random. After all, it only ever rains in England, does it not! And now one disease after another crosses the Channel and threatens livelihoods! This is how many people express their sentiments and I find that it hurts to hear it. I think of how in England I had often heard unkind remarks about Germany, and now the tables are turned and I am again on the receiving end of it. Twice I am refused hospitality when people find that I have walked from England—the fear and anxiety sits deep and goes beyond rational judgement.

But there are also many farms where I am made welcome. The first is the Terrenhof, on the eastern border of the German-speaking part of Belgium. On that day I walk through solitary woodland and often wonder whether I am walking in the right direction. There has been a constant light drizzle throughout the day, which accentuates all the different hues of greens of the mosses and undergrowth and makes the vegetation sparkle like precious jewels. It is there, too, that I look directly into the eyes of a noble deer for what seems like an eternity, while it returns my gaze! I have never experienced anything like it before. Through the eyes of the deer I am transported into a different world, into the soul of the animal world whose destiny is so incredibly intertwined with our own; and yet we often fail in our responsibilities towards them!

My path continues through further stretches of woodland with many fallen trees glowing in the almost psychedelic colours of decomposition. The pine trees are decorated with raindrop pearls.

At last I reach the farm and after all this solitude I find myself surrounded by a crowd of children and teenagers. As they speak German I can communicate freely with them. Here I have the first of many long conversations with the farmers about the terrible scenes in England. I hear of the fight for survival to which small farmers are subjected, how they often live on the breadline and are forced to work from dawn to dusk with hardly a break, and often with no holidays or even weekend leave.

Solitude

It is in those deep forests of the Ardennes that I experience a feeling of solitude such as I have never known before in my life. Solitude is to be my constant companion for the rest of my journey, and accompanies me into the woods of Luxembourg and into the forested hills in Germany of Hunsrück, Taunus, Vogelsberg, Rhone, Thüringer Wald, Frankenwald, Vogtland, Erzgebirge, Elbsandsteingebirge and finally Bohemia. She will accompany me now until I reach Prague.

What is she like, this travel companion of mine, and why do I become aware of her only now?

I think she was a gift of the forests. Never before have I experienced the forest as now, even though I grew up in the foothills of the Black Forest in Germany. But the Black Forest, despite its name, is tame in comparison to the wilderness that I encounter here. These are woods as painted by Mathias Grünewald in the sixteenth century. He was truly named, for Grünewald means 'green wood'. The trees are covered in many-coloured mosses and lichens, and amidst them rise great rocks. Solitude appears in these surroundings, and as she enters my soul my eyes open further, and I look into the unfathomable depth of nature and my own being. Mighty sounds of sobbing emerge from within me; I resist and beg and at the same time every fibre of my being is longing to fully open myself to this new experience, to say 'yes' to it, as I recognize that all my life I have been waiting for it. I have known loneliness before, to be sure, but that was wholly different. In those times I was alone, but not by choice, and had been miserable and unhappy on account of it or had covered it up somehow. Now I open myself fully, embrace and became one with Solitude. And I know then that in the future I will miss her terribly when she goes, when I have to return to my former life. She has caused me, at the same time, immeasurable pain and tremendous joy, and I recognize this as a big theme in my life. This helps me understand many riddles of my biography which previously eluded me. Now I have the opportunity to fully experience the gifts of this being, Solitude, something that is almost impossible to achieve in the daily life of a culture that offers so much diversion and distraction, relentlessly so, and thus prevents this profound meeting with and facing up to oneself.

I gave thanks to the forests for this gift. In England you don't often find such forests. I had to return to the country of my birth to be able to receive it—the land of the deep dark woods of fairy tales, home to all kinds of beings, malevolent and helpful, those who set obstacles on the path and those who put you to the test, where danger lurks but also salvation.

Since my encounter with Solitude I have become much more silent, more peaceful, humbler and more vulnerable. I begin to speak to her, ask her to help me, ask for her advice, and tell her what is happening, my thoughts and feelings. Rarely does she respond, but when she does it is never an easy answer; it means that I have to overcome something, that I have to take a new step.

Sometimes Solitude sends rewards, as on 13 March. It proves to be the most taxing day so far; I have lost my way several times and am beginning to think I cannot continue.

And then, having climbed to the summit of a big hill in Luxembourg on the border with Germany, a radiant rainbow bridge appears, spanning the river that forms the border between the two countries. Later, when I finally arrive at the goat farm where I am to spend the night, and where I am given the most delicious goat's cheese I have ever tasted, I bear witness to a glorious sunset—one that could have been lifted straight from a Turner painting.

The day is followed by a clear and sparkling night sky, strewn with stars.

I am now in the westernmost part of Germany and am starting on the long stretch across the heart of the country. My journey takes me in the direction of Echternach, a medieval bishop's town, through a landscape of bizarre rock formations with names such as 'Devil's Dungeon' and 'Devil's Gorge', past Roman relics and along very steep and adventurous pathways that make progress hard going. I walk past a curious rock pool in Enzen that seems very old but I later learn was constructed in the 1860s on the initiative of the local vicar, who wanted to start a positive project at a time of great unemployment.

This is the gateway to my country of origin, Germany. The greatest part of my pilgrimage will lead me right through its heart.

Roman Germany

My further journey presents some obstacles. I am again following signposts for the European long-distance path E3 that at one point leads me to a roaring brook swollen by winter rains, the ferocity of the water having made the footbridge collapse. It is impossible to cross and I have to make a great detour to get to the other side. This happens a second time on the same day, and I have to add still more miles to the journey and even leave my marked path altogether to reach my destination. I encounter yet another problem as I discover that there are no footpath maps to be had in the village because it is winter. Who in their right mind goes walking in winter?

So I have no choice but to board a local bus to take me into the ancient Roman city of Trier, where I buy my map and after a while return by bus to the same spot to continue my pilgrimage. The bus driver scolds me on account of my muddy boots, adding to my feeling of being a tramp in the eyes of the world, an outcast existing on the margins of society. It is perhaps because of this that I find myself very receptive to the strange mood emanating from Trier, a city strongly characterized by its Roman past. I visit the ruins of the ancient bathhouses, the amphitheatre, the Porta Nigra, the old Roman bridges, the basilica and the cathedral. I feel a rising melancholy; I feel lonely and sad, as well as somehow strangely inert. There is nothing of levity in this architecture at all; it is given over to the laws of gravity and together with the leaden sky and the polluted air gives rise to the feeling of being imprisoned.

As I leave Trier I pass the curious Roman column of Igel, quite by surprise, as it stands there in the middle of a neat and tidy village in the suburbs. It is covered in carvings of battle scenes and various figures, and is completely at odds with the well-kept buildings around it. I see a plaque that tells me that Goethe himself stood there in 1792 and admired its artistry. Soon after this I reach this area's extensive vineyards, which are also after all a legacy of the Romans, and give this countryside its character; and I can again look into the far distances.

From this point, the E3 follows the old Roman path called the Limes for more than 100 km, until Saalburg near Frankfurt, and even out in nature a sense of the heaviness of Roman culture prevails. And now the days are marked by the return of severe winter weather. I drag myself along in downcast mood through difficult territory with a lot of mud underfoot and a nagging headache, and I have to admit to myself that I have once again reached a low point on my journey. The relentless rain has really got under my skin.

Sometimes, at the end of such a day, the evening brings a certain redemption with it, as between Greimerrath and Oberlöstern when I reach the chapel dedicated to Nikolaus von der Flü, a hermit, originally from Switzerland, who in 1467 left his family to follow a call from God. He lived for 20 years without food or drink, wore no shoes or cap, summer or winter. Here, the heavy clouds part to show the mist rising down in the valley and I find myself as if set down in a painting by Caspar David Friedrich! But soon enough the rain returns—and persists.

March 22 is supposed to be the beginning of spring, but it doesn't feel like it. I am walking past a remarkable Celtic fortress, probably the site of battle with the Romans. Patches of wet, slippery snow and freezing damp weather stay with me throughout that day until I reach another farm, this time with horses, Hof Birkenau. My friendly host is an artist as well as a farmer, gives courses on the therapeutic aspects of horse riding, and studies Sufism, Native American mythology and psychotherapy. Her farm was built at the end of World War II as a place for refugees from eastern Germany, and has now been transformed by her skills. She invites me to stay a second night to have a break from the trials of the weather.

Foot-and-Mouth Disease

It is 26 March, and I am walking from Berschweiler to See-
bach in a very rural area, through lonely valleys and mountains; the day brings me a lot of climbing up, coming down
and climbing up again. I visit the castle of Dhaun, enfolded in
the steep slopes of the Simmertal. Until then I have really
been enjoying myself, but now I begin to have a strange
feeling of dread as I again have no proper destination, no
address to go to, and I cannot find any signs of lodgings in
these lonely hamlets. In the end, not knowing what else to do,
I turn to my invisible companion with a plea for help. In this
way a strange set of circumstances is set in motion, providing
me with the most unusual lodgings to date: I knock on
somebody's house and nobody answers, and as I turn to leave
again I see an old man by the window beckoning and so I
enter the living room where he is seated by a table eating
apples. He is waiting for his wife and cannot give me an
answer to my request until she returns. So I sit down as well
and wait with him. As she enters her home and listens to my
question, she is quick to answer: 'What makes you think that
you can stay here? This is not an inn and I cannot understand
how you can think of such a thing!'

I feel most acutely embarrassed and want the floor to open
and swallow me up.

But then she stops herself, perhaps remembering that,
really, there are no lodgings to be found for a good many
miles. Her husband mumbles: 'Oh do let her stay!'

She explains to me that she was planning to go out this evening to her women friends and felt reluctant to cancel. I assure her that I would be perfectly happy for her to do so and to keep company with the old man. On hearing this she most warmly offers hospitality and invites me to supper, after which I watch television with her husband and answer his questions, which come at lengthy intervals. In this way I find out, gradually, that he knows all the farms within a certain radius of here because in the past he used to go from farm to farm trimming the hooves of the animals. Meanwhile we watch the horror scenes of the animal funeral pyres on the television screen—burning mountains of flesh, smoke over the landscape, scenes like a country at war.

The following morning I take fond leave of these two people, who managed to overcome an initial inhibition and allow a total stranger into their house. When I offer some payment the farmer's wife turns it down and says that she only wishes me to send a postcard when I reach my destination. 'And if I had known beforehand, I would have asked the press to come and write about your pilgrimage!' By now she is quite overcome with this unusual incident that has interrupted their quiet and predictable existence in this remote corner of the Hunsrück.

The next farm I visit is managed by Johannes, a fairly young biodynamic farmer. On the way I cross the Soonwald, a woodland of many legends and stories. I can almost imagine a gnome peeping from behind an old moss-covered tree stump, and would not be surprised to see a ring of fairies dancing in an open glade.

I find my host Johannes working on the farm and his four children fending for themselves in the kitchen. The eldest girl, of about 16, tells me that their mother now lives elsewhere and that she herself is in charge of the younger children. The littlest is about 4 years old. It is already quite late at night when Johannes returns from the stables, and yet he still has time to meet me and enter into conversation. He is deeply concerned at what is going on in England, and ponders the spiritual significance of this tragedy. He speaks to me of his own belief in the *group soul* of the animals in his charge, and how he tries to get in touch with it prior to slaughter, asking for permission—in the same way, I have read, as some nomadic tribes in Africa and elsewhere. Slaughter then becomes a ritual; it is done with reverence and respect for the animal. The senseless scenes of slaughter in England are the absolute opposite of this. He also speaks of the possibility that this horror could repeat itself in Germany, but he is trying not to give in to fear. He could never consent to a slaughter order issued by the authorities, and he would do everything in his power to resist it.

Johannes also tells me of his deep connection with the particular piece of land that he works. He bought this farm a few years previously because he felt connected with the area, even though he originates from the Baden district, not far in fact from the town where I grew up. He explores the forests of the Hunsrück on horseback, and prefers its wilderness to the neatly kept farms of Baden. He goes on to tell me about a life-changing journey the previous year, when he took up a friend's invitation to visit Morocco and the Atlas Mountains. He compares the inner experiences of this trip to my pilgrimage and understands why I needed to do it. This conversation late into the night echoes on for me as I resume my travelling, after a rest-day on this special farm. Johannes helps me with my further planning, and with obtaining maps, which has continued to be a problem since crossing the German border.

My next walking day takes me to the Rhine, and I relish the first sighting of it from high upon the castle-crowned ridges that fall steeply to the banks of this mighty river. I feel my heart beat faster and wonder at the different river that I encounter as compared to the slow and sluggish waters of the Rhine of my childhood district, where its bed is much wider and the surrounding fields lush and flat, heavy with crops. Here the vicinity of the river is full of drama and romance as I approach Rheinböllen and Bacharach. My joy culminates in taking lodgings in one of those proud castles, which now serves as a youth hostel. My heart is filled with the joy and expectation of what the next day might bring when I cross the Rhine—always an important marker between two countries.

At first the crossing proves to be quite a difficult under-taking as the river is swollen from the recent rains, and the ferries are not operating everywhere. As a result I have to walk for quite a few miles along the tarmac road, alongside roaring traffic, to reach a larger ferry to take me across.

On reaching the other side I find myself, significantly, in a different district. The day before I wanted to buy the map for my onward journey and was told that I had to wait until I crossed the river since they did not sell maps in one district for the other!

The western part of the Taunus is like the Hunsrück—full of wild and rugged valleys, steep hillsides and deep, lonely woodland. I chance upon the solitary ruin of an old castle tucked away among the trees and swathed with flimsy clouds of haze. I look at it as if in trance; a distant memory tries to rise to the surface and does not quite succeed. But my soul receives a message, and I want to weep for joy and happiness, for pain and sadness, gain and loss, all rolled in one. It is hard to tear myself away from this spot, but I need to continue. I walk along some lively brooks and the recent rain has washed the leaves of the trees, which glisten in the afternoon sunlight.

This is my last day in this blessed wilderness as I am now approaching the vast sprawl of Wiesbaden, Mainz and Frankfurt. Although the E3 does not actually run through these cities, the character of the woodland is now utterly changed because of their proximity. It is monotonous, and very well sign-posted; and Sunday hikers, dogs, horses, joggers and cyclists fill broad, gravelled paths.

All day long I walk through city woodland. Everywhere I meet people. I am not used to it. Then an unexpected sound reaches my ear: I hear music, a trumpet playing every now and then, and melodies of folk songs that I remember from my childhood. I absorb the sounds deeply—I have not listened to music for such a long time. It makes me happy, and the woodland somehow more attractive.

Towards evening I reach a hilltop with a viewing tower. I debate whether or not to climb it to sample the view; it is getting late and my hosts for the night have asked me to come early in the evening, as they want to go out later. I am already getting a bit pressed for time, but the clear, crisp light of the early sunset beckons and I cannot resist it. I have been amongst trees all day long without a single opportunity to look into the distance.

Imagine my surprise to find the trumpeter on top of this tower! I look into a friendly, old face with clear blue eyes framed by silver hair. He has a hearty laugh and is full of interest in my story. I tell him how much it meant to me during my walking today to hear his music! He tells his story, too. Many years of his life he spent working on a conveyor belt in a factory to feed his family and finally to be able to afford his own humble cottage. Originally he hailed from Sudetenland, the eastern part of Germany annexed to Poland, which he remembers with fondness. Then he points to the panoramic view around the tower and exclaims that he would never wish to travel abroad as all the beauty he can possibly want is spread out here in front of us! He can name every single hill. In all his factory years he spent what free time he had playing the trumpet, self-taught; this is what kept him sane. Since his retirement he has got into the habit of driving to all the various viewing towers, when the weather is fine, to play his trumpet in celebration of the glorious country that he now calls his home, and to bring joy to others. This is what gives meaning to his life. We take our leave, but not before he invites me to visit him at his house in a village a few days' journey from here. I make my way down the hill to the accompaniment of his trumpet and look forward to my visit to his house, glad to be able to meet with him again.

The next couple of days are hard work once more, through ailing woodland, which makes me feel heavy and inert. Everything seems given over to gravity. I walk along the Limes, the old Roman boundary wall. I feel sapped of energy and all my joy and enthusiasm seems to be gone. On top of that it has started to rain again and I shiver in the damp, clammy air, and cannot get warm for the rest of the day.

In this mood I reach the Saalburg, which is a reconstructed Roman Camp, now turned into a museum of Roman military artefacts. Its heavy walls and square buildings seem impenetrable and cold, surrounded by brooding darkness.

This is my meeting place with Astrid, a woman who had written to me and invited me to stay with her in Frankfurt. This city was the scene of three very difficult months of homelessness for me, after I had run away from home in my mid-teens. I was now to receive a very special gift of hospitality in the very same city, with a woman whom I have never met and who seems completely familiar to me from the very first moment. This is one of those rare encounters with another human being where you immediately get to a deep place in a conversation, which is relevant, urgent and supremely meaningful to both people. And then she insists that I sleep in her bed whilst she takes the sofa! Here I stay for a few days, to be lazy, rest my tired bones and let the rain pass. I read, and take walks with Astrid when she comes home from work, and we continue our conversation. We have so much to say to each other! As I prepare to continue my journey, she fixes me up with some more addresses and packs so much food into my bag that I will be blessed with treats for quite a few days to come.

On 7 April I reach the house of my trumpeter. First I meet his wife, who regards me in a way similar to the farmer's wife who found me with her husband in the living room. It turns out that her husband has not properly told her I am coming, and she seems a little put out. He himself will not be home until evening.

But soon, over a cup of tea, she warms to me and confides that, really, she and her family are a little fed up with all this trumpet playing; they hear nothing else. But that does not diminish her fondness for him. When at last her husband arrives home we spend a lovely evening together, talking until well into the night.

Three generations live under this one roof; I meet his daughter and her baby. We study the map together and I am quizzed about the route which I plan to take the next day. They want to know what time and where I will be stopping for lunch! We take fond leave of each other in the morning.

Unbeknown to me, my trumpeter secretly drives to the town I aim to reach by lunchtime, and waits for me in the marketplace. As soon as he spots me coming round the corner he starts playing his trumpet, announcing my arrival and greeting me like the Queen of Sheba, to the amazement of the people gathered there! We embrace like long-lost friends, and for a while this scene is far more interesting to the tourists than the finely decorated, half-timbered houses for which this place is famous.

New Meetings

Often on this journey people have asked: 'How come your husband allows you to do this?' Maybe they wonder whether our marriage is ailing. I myself also ask this question. At my departure we had been married for 24 years, and raised three children who are now about to embark on their own lives. It has certainly not been an 'easy marriage' because we are two very different people, in temperament and constitution. There have been very difficult times where we had to ask ourselves whether there was more to the marriage than raising our children. And yet as often as we plummeted into those depths we always found the way back out again. Now we have come to a time when our marriage is no longer needed for the sake of the children. We have the opportunity to look at each other anew, and to ponder this question in earnest and with utter honesty.

It is the theme of my pilgrimage to look at all aspects of my life anew, to get distance, quite literally, and to take leave, to let go and shed unwanted ballast. I set out on this journey to allow the unexpected to happen, to get to the bottom of certain riddles of my biography, to find clarity and a new vision.

A deep encounter between two people is the greatest riddle. Sometimes you feel the aeons of past time that bring their signature to this meeting. The encounter is mightier and far greater than the two people concerned, who look into each other's eyes, slowly explore each other's scent and touch, who gradually reach into the deeper recesses of each other and recognize who is there. But is it not up to us what we make of the relationship? Whatever mysteries bring about a significant encounter, it is up to us to forge it into a meaningful relationship and to discover the greater meaning behind it.

Of course, we have also had happy times together in sharing our lives, when we rejoiced together, when we learned something new, explored new horizons. Our life has been simple; money has never been plentiful, but we always found an imaginative way to manage, and our holidays were spent close to nature, which we both love. Our children have grown into splendid young people who tackle life with great enthusiasm and still like coming back to visit often.

Life is like a canvas. The picture happens whilst it is being painted. The path is created by walking it. The colours move and direct the painting, then the painter takes over and directs the colours for a time; a dialogue happens; there is constant movement, weighing up, balancing out. I would like there to be movement, potential, unpredictability right to the end of my life. In that moment when I have the feeling that something is set in stone, taken for granted, determined to be as it is from now on, I turn away. This feeling clips my wings, stifles my creativity, freezes my spirit.

I love my marriage. Perhaps these are strange words to choose to express it, but they bring me closer to what I want to say. My marriage is very precious to me and irreplaceable. In order to keep it precious I need to feel that there is movement. I would not be able to bear a marriage that has become stale and stagnant—the thought of it fills me with repugnance. It is precisely because of the many transformations that our marriage has undergone that it has grown so dear to me. I have also grown very fond of the man to whom I am married, and realize that he recognizes the deepest core of me. It is why he gave his 'permission' for me to go on this pilgrimage, helped me organize it (because that's not my strong point), and has inwardly accompanied it all the way. What greater gift could I have wished for?

And now we are going to meet up. We planned this before I left, but it began to look impossible to arrange it because of the foot-and-mouth outbreak in England. People were not really supposed to leave the country and those who absolutely had to were subjected to a rigorous disinfection procedure on entering another country. The conference that he was due to attend had at first been cancelled due to these restrictions, then it seemed possible again and I finally got news that he was coming after all. The conference was to take place in the very community where I had my next lodgings; we could not have planned it better if we tried. Our meeting place is in the Wetterau, a flat stretch of landscape with fields and orchards lying between the Taunus and Vogelsberg. I reach the picturesque castle of Münzenberg and there I meet my husband, among the narrow cobbled streets.

There I see him—in the meantime he has grown a beard! We look into each other's eyes as if seeing the other for the first time, and I find myself inwardly asking the same questions. Who are you? Where do you come from? Where is your path leading you? We again feel the inevitability of our encounter, for a brief moment. It continues to be a riddle and a task. There is further potential to be explored; there is room for creativity; there is movement. Yes, you are my life's companion, my partner! And then the everyday persona takes over and we need to attend to practical matters. Bernard is not allowed to stay on the farm, having just travelled from England, and the community finds some alternative accommodation for us.

Bernard accompanies me for two days through the Vogelsberg. This is the area where the Brothers Grimm collected most of their fairy tales 200 years ago. The first night we spend in a splendid château divided into flats, one of which we are welcome to use despite my host's absence. Bernard is not a man of many words, and after we have exchanged the main news we walk largely in silence. I am glad for that this time; I am so used to silence now, and need it. The rhythm of our walking and the rustle of the leaves in the woods are company enough, until a sudden hailstorm interrupts our walking and I realize that I am much more hardened to the weather now than he. It used to be the other way round! The next day he is too tired to come with me, which amuses me somewhat.

Our next host has organized an evening gathering of farmers' wives, where I am invited to give an account of my travels. I arrive as if in a dream and wonder what on earth to talk about. As soon as I begin, the story tells itself and I listen to it with amazement!

The last stretch with Bernard brings us to another community in Herbstein-Schlechtenwegen, one of the addresses that Astrid, my host in Frankfurt, had arranged for me. Our host turns out to be a very old acquaintance of Bernard's from his first workplace after leaving school, which was on a farmstead in the north of Germany! This is another of those seemingly strange coincidences of my journey.

At this point news reaches me that I need to interrupt my journey and visit my (birth) family. We are approaching the

Easter weekend. Bernard takes his leave to return to England by plane and I think to myself: *All this distance that you travel now in the air, I have walked it! It was lovely to have this time with you but now I need to continue again by myself.*

What follows is a story I wrote for my mother a few years before. It was inspired by a painting by Rembrandt called *The Man in Armour*, sometimes also referred to as *Alexander the Great* or *Mars*. It shows a portrait of a man with touchingly feminine features and attributes, such as wearing an earring.

The reason why I wish to include this story in my account is because at this point in my journey I had to make a decision against my wishes to spend time with my parents, with whom I had a complex relationship. I am mainly going to describe the encounter between my father and myself, as my mother was in hospital just then. For most of my adult life it has been impossible to have conversations of a deeper nature with my mother due to our particular family constellation. The story represents one of the conversations I wish I could have had with my mother.

Shemron (dedicated to my mother)

Shemron had always been a soldier, and he knew no fear. He also was without a home, forever restless, travelling, a wanderer. His features showed the traces of the many paths he had travelled; his eyes spoke of courage and adventure. He had traversed many a mountain range and visited their colourful inhabitants; he knew their customs and had celebrated their festivals with them. He had also crossed many oceans and encountered the inhabitants of remote islands. And yet some-

times a faint, distant memory touched his heart and reminded him of a time when life had been different. Shemron never quite let this memory come fully into consciousness.

One day, again, the language of his heart told Shemron of another journey he still needed to accomplish, a different journey from all the others. He began to long increasingly for solitude, and sought out moments when he could take counsel with himself. And through this solitude he became utterly lost to the world, without memory, without a past, without an image of a future. And this is why he could not remember at all how he had arrived in the small and dimly lit room of a tower. He was clothed in his trusty armour, with his shield and his sword. The sun was about to set, sending the last rays through the window, transforming the light. He stood by the window, immersed in his thoughts, and the light gilded his armour and his helmet—he became one with the sun.

Later he could not tell how long he had been standing there; had it been a minute or an hour, had years gone by and centuries passed? This change was wrought by the very last rays of the sun as they had touched him. There was now no going back. Never again would he be known as Shemron the soldier. And yet why did he feel his courage waning? Why did he recoil? He who had never known fear found that his knees were shaking and his heartbeat seemed to shatter his breast.

A mighty memory rose up in him and he felt himself carried by a current that he could not control. A mighty wind swung him through the air in spirals. Further and further he was carried, through the many aeons of his own being. And even though he knew that this power originated from a very distant past, he could feel that he was being carried towards his future.

When the wind stopped, Shemron felt himself completely

devoid of strength, and the leaden weariness of all his travels descended upon him. He crept into a corner of the room. Everything contracted within him and his gaze was directed inwards—he felt himself small, so small. He would not have minded disappearing altogether. At that moment he beheld a small white dove that flew down onto the window sill. Her feathers emanated a strange light that did not seem to be of this world. Shemron rose and looked at the dove for a long time. What beauty in its simplicity!

A mighty longing awoke in his heart. He wanted to be the dove, to spread his wings and overcome the earth's heaviness! The dove will take me to my true home, he thought, the home that I nearly forgot! Slowly he advanced towards the dove, very slowly, shyly and carefully, fearing that she would vanish at any moment. Behind him spread the star-studded sky. Never before had Shemron felt so close to the diamond splendour of the stars. The moon stood silently and traced a sharp chalice into the velvet darkness, carrying the host. Gossamer-fine, silvery clouds were carried across the sky by the wind and arranged themselves around the moon sickle in gentle rainbow colours. Below he felt the dark and silent earth.

In the tower he felt himself to be exactly midway between heaven and earth. The serene beauty of the starry night and the scent of the pine forest below him touched him deeply in his inner being. His longing gave way to deep gratefulness, and with it came a silent strength. From there he could feel his being expand, and he beheld all the mountains he had ever crossed, all the oceans he had travelled, all the valleys he had ever visited, the people he had loved or fought in this former life. The feeling of compassion merged with the newly felt gratefulness, and now he knew that he loved the earth in the same way as the heavens.

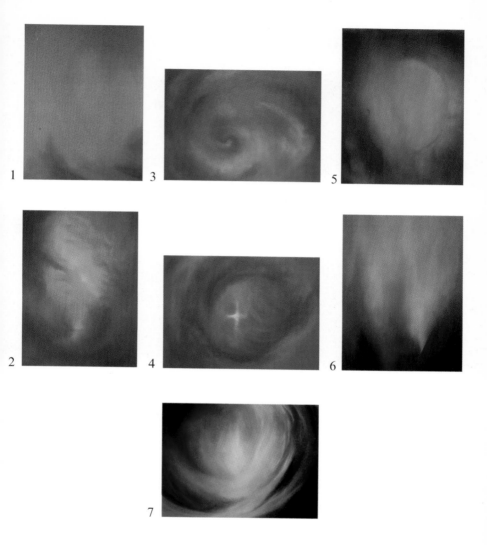

The Foundation Stone Meditation

Human Soul!
You live in the limbs
Which bear you through the world of space
Within the flowing ocean of the spirit:
Practise *spirit re-cognition*
In depths of soul,
Where in the wielding will
Of world creating
The individual I
Comes to being
In the I of God;
And you will truly *live*
In your body's cosmic being.

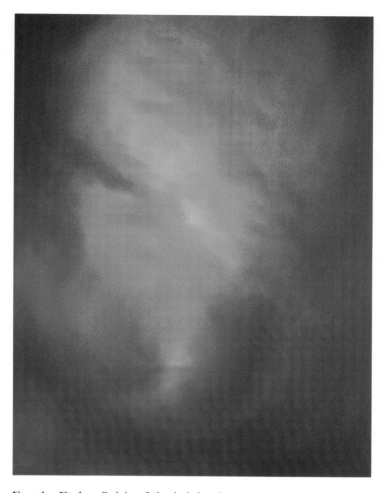

For the Father Spirit of the heights is present
In world depths begetting existence:
Spirits of Strength!
May there ring forth from the heights
The call re-echoed in the depths;
Proclaiming:
Humankind is born of God.
The elemental spirits hear it
In east, west, north, south:
*May hu*man beings *hear it!*

Human Soul!
You live in the beat of heart and lung
Which leads you through the rhythm of time
Into the realm of your own soul's feeling.
Practise *spirit presence*
In soul composure,
Where the weaving deeds
Of universal becoming
Unite
The individual I
With the I of the World;
And you will truly *feel*
In the active life of your soul.

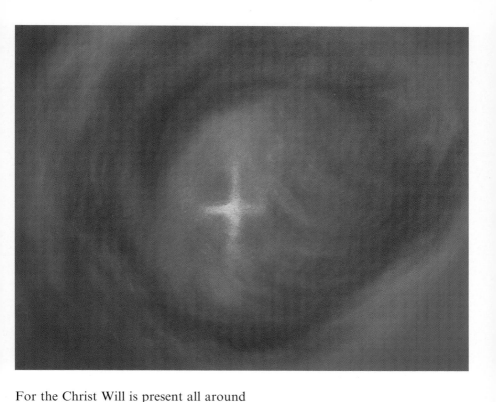

For the Christ Will is present all around
In world rhythms shedding grace on our souls;
Spirits of Light!
May what is formed by the west
Have been quickened in the light of the east;
Proclaiming:
In Christ death becomes life.
The elemental spirits hear it
In east, west, north, south:
*May hu*man beings *hear it!*

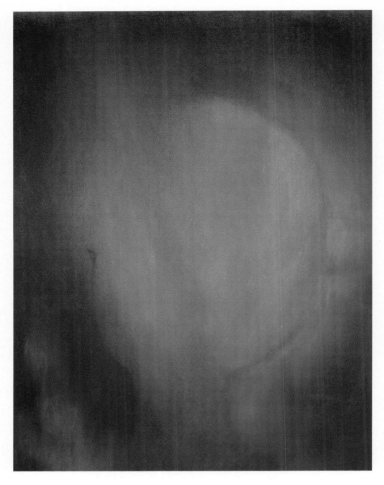

Human Soul!
You live in the stillness of the head
Which from the founts of eternity
Discloses for you cosmic thoughts:
Practise *spirit beholding*
In thought calm,
Where the eternal aims of Gods
Give the light of spirit worlds
To the individual I
For will in freedom.
And you will truly *think*
In the founts of your human spirit.

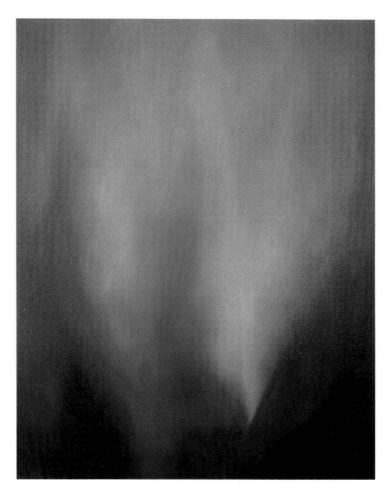

For the Spirit's cosmic thoughts are present
In world existence begging for light;
Spirits of Soul!
May there ascend from the depths
The plea heard in the heights;
Proclaiming:
In the Spirit's cosmic thoughts the soul will awaken.
The elemental spirits hear it
In east, west, north, south:
*May hu*man beings *hear it!*

At the turning of time
Cosmic Spirit Light descended
Into the earthly stream of being;
Darkness of night
Had run its course;
The light of day
Shone forth in human souls:
Light
That gives warmth
To poor shepherds' hearts,
Light
That enlightens
The wise heads of kings.

God-given light,
Christ Sun
Give warmth
To our hearts;
Give light
To our heads;
That what we found
From our hearts
What we guide
From our heads
Will be good.

Solitude

Crown of Thorns

Relics from Karlstein: a piece of the Cross

Relics from Karlstein: the holy Lance

The impulse to go on a journey

Inside Karlstein

This is how it happened that Shemron took up travelling again. Only this time it was a completely different journey. Shemron again mingled with the people, but nobody recognized him without his armour. He wore the garments of poverty, a simple sack linen. Instead of his sword he carried a pilgrim's staff.

From time to time people would tell each other that they had met a lonely wanderer and given him hospitality, and that they had felt a blessing emanating from him as he had taken leave—a blessing that stayed with them always. Outwardly not much had changed in their lives, but their gaze would now look differently upon the world. They found that they had the gift of story-telling, something that they had not been able to do before, and they found that many people came to listen to the stories. They were new stories, such as had never been told before.

It took a long time before these people found one another and discovered what they had in common, namely, that they had each taken in a stranger from the road, not for very long and without exchanging too many words, and that the stranger had looked at them with a gaze that had touched them in their deepest core. After the stranger departed they each promised themselves to remain faithful to this new openness of heart which his gaze had kindled in them. They could never again speak a word of untruth, of pride or of jealousy, without suffering the most excruciating pain. And when after a time they became wholly imbued by their faithfulness, they found a tremendous, quiet joy in their hearts that never wavered no matter what life brought to them.

These people, men and women from far-flung places, eventually found one another. Often they talked together about this lonely stranger. They spoke about him with great reverence.

The connection they felt with one another grew ever stronger over the years. They made an effort to meet regularly, albeit not as often as they would have wished; they helped one another in times of need; they rejoiced with each other at times of celebration. But they knew that the last and final building stone to their community was still missing.

Many years passed. Those same people who had met the stranger in their youth sat in the circle with grey hair and bent backs. Many amongst them had already crossed the threshold into another existence, and yet still the community increased in size as new, younger people joined.

And so it happened that they gathered together once again. There was storytelling and exchanging of news; they sang and ate their meals together. The tables were laden with the choicest food, the specialities of the many different countries they hailed from. There were exotic fruits and rare wines and the tables were decorated with beautiful flowers. A new guest entered the hall. Whoever saw him rose from their seat to greet him. They noticed the deep furrows in his features, traces of deep thinking, traces of deep sorrows. He was led to the tables and invited to partake in the meal. When he arose to take his leave he was urged to stay. So he began to speak to them. His words came only slowly, hesitantly, but he spoke with a clarity and warmth, and everyone felt personally addressed by him in the deepest recesses of their hearts; they felt his gaze met theirs the whole time he was speaking. Few amongst them could make sense of his words, and those who did could not entirely piece them together after he had left, but all could feel the resonance of those words.

He left the company silent and in astonishment. Each one of them now carried a treasure in their heart, and a resolve to stay together from now on as a community, even beyond their life-times and in the centuries to come. They promised one another to keep the sacred memory of this holy gathering, which had now found the completion they had been looking for. They knew for certain that they would meet him again and that he would speak to them once more.

They became the keepers of the voice of the heart.

Easter

Maybe it was because of Bernard's and my all-too-brief meeting that it hits me so hard, but all of a sudden the distance between me and my former life, my family, my work, colleagues, friends and my children seems huge. On reaching the town where I grew up, and where my parents still live, I fall into a big depression. After the third day I have an ugly exchange of words with my father and the pain of my dysfunctional childhood comes over me. I perceive the marriage between my parents as a trap from which they have not been able to free themselves. How many years have I tried to work through this pain, to integrate those experiences somehow and, I had thought, to change them? Now I see a nothingness, a great emptiness. Nothing is left of what I thought I had achieved in my own process of transformation, just nothing. I am the same way I have always been: bad, ugly, caught up in my own concerns, and trapped within myself, with no possibility of escape. It's not possible to escape—that much at least I did learn. I plunge into deep despair, because I cannot see any way out—just as in my childhood. The worst feeling was always that there is simply no way out. Like a nightmare when you are being pursued and all escape routes are blocked.

The full misery of the parts of me that have not been changed stands in front of me now. I have no protection; I am completely exposed. At first I feel the blackest darkness, which is followed by a cold and glaring light that makes it impossible to find peace. Impenetrable darkness and cutting light alternate continuously, and I find myself torn between the two, fractured into tiny pieces. It is like the picture in the Isenheim altar that I know so very well: St Anthony is thrust to the ground, surrounded by terrible beasts and demons who attack him, tear at him, rip at his garment in an attempt to overpower him. Above him is the burning ruin of a house being destroyed by devils. Still further up are icy cold mountains, in terrible contrast to the burning fire. It is said that St Anthony cried out at this moment: 'My God, my God, why hast thou forsaken me?' He is not aware of the presence of the Archangel Michael who, surrounded by a halo of light, hastens to his aid and enters the fight, not with the sharp edge of his sword but, turning it around, with the hilt, which forms a cross. All this St Anthony will only later find out, when the fight is already done and he has an encounter with one who is older and wiser than himself. And I remember now the nightmarish dream I had about the ugly, slimy being.

When a personal drama happens we all, always, partake in the much bigger drama of humanity. This is what connects us—our suffering, fighting, errors, downfalls and our coming up again. There are philosophies and religions that seek to eliminate suffering. My question to their followers is: What happens then to my connection with all other human beings who do not follow this particular path? My brother's suffering is also truly my own. This is Christ's teaching, whose feast of Resurrection is today. He has himself walked the path of suffering and sustained the wounds, inflicted by other human beings, and transformed them into new organs of perception. Grünewald painted this, too, in the mighty panel that depicts the scene of the Crucifixion and then the Resurrection.

Today is Easter Sunday, the feast of Resurrection. In the meantime I have totally sunk back into myself and fail to hear the church bells ringing. The time is up, I can no longer celebrate Easter this year. I can only see my own grimaces, my guilt and my lack of love.

Brother Max

A few days after this terrible low-point I resume my journey. Inside I feel like a wounded soldier. My soul is still frozen, pervaded by a feeling of emptiness and greyness, the exhaustion after the fight. I arrive in a small town (Lauterbach) and walk the streets rather aimlessly, trying to pick up the thread of my pilgrimage. I don't seem to succeed. I am overcome with a feeling of paralysis. I have been defeated.

The next day I grow into my walking rhythm again which has helped me over quite a number of difficulties before. I am grateful for it as I feel smitten by wounds that will take a long while to heal.

I read the names of the footpaths. One is called Jacob's path, the route that would have been taken by pilgrims from the East to go to Santiago de Compostella. Another is named after the Brothers Grimm, the collectors of fairy tales. But there is a constant drizzle of rain, and it is cold and gloomy. After two days like this I reach the old Bishop's town of Fulda and I see the snow-covered hills of the Rhone district ahead of me, which I will have to scale over the coming days and where I will reach the former border to communist Germany, the Iron Curtain. The previous day I telephoned ahead and spoke to a monk at one of the monasteries in Fulda, to ask for hospitality. At first I was turned down. The monk explained to me that they are in the middle of some building work and therefore cannot receive visitors. But he continued to listen to me and at last he said, 'Well, if you are a pilgrim then you

must come and stay here!' Upon my arrival I meet the monk
with whom I had spoken; he has come to the gate to greet me.
He shows me to my room, which is very simple, even austere.
On the table I see a small Easter decoration, a bottle of water
and a tiny sweet.

After I am refreshed, Brother Max returns and escorts me
to the refectory to have supper with the monks. He introduces
me to them with words of welcome, and afterwards invites me
to an evening celebration at which he will officiate for people
outside the monastery. It is a Bible Evening. Today they are
reading the passage of doubting Thomas, who needed to
place his hands into the wounds of the Christ in order to
believe in his Resurrection. Many of the visitors express their
identification with this figure of doubting Thomas. It is a
truly modern dilemma—we rely on our earthly senses even
when we want to approach spiritual matters. Only after
everyone who wants to has spoken does Brother Max offer
his insights. He speaks about touch, and how we use this
word also in a supersensible way when we say that we are
touched by an encounter with somebody. We can touch one
another with our souls, without any physical touch, and be
deeply enriched by it. Then Brother Max spreads a cloth on
the floor and proceeds to celebrate the Eucharist, kneeling in
front of us. The cloth becomes the altar. Brother Max is not a
priest now, he becomes one with his brothers and sisters. He
shares out the bread and the wine and then speaks a blessing
to each one. I am invited to come and partake also.

I don't know why this scene imprints itself so deeply into
my soul. It seems that time stands still, and it is one of those
moments when the veil between this world and another
becomes thinner for me and allows a glimpse into a far-off

time of great significance which I cannot grasp with my rational mind. I feel so deeply accepted, not only by the human beings present at this moment, but also by unseen beings who witness this event, too. Nothing else could have stilled the deeply aching heart with which I entered the monastery, and given healing balsam to my wounded soul.

After the visitors have gone he asks me about my journey. In particular he wants to know where I am going to stay the following nights, so I have to admit to him that I actually don't know. I do have some addresses further on, but not for the next two nights. On hearing this, Brother Max goes to the office and phones around until he has the assurance of a nunnery and another monastery to give me shelter on my way. The next morning he again escorts me to the gate. He tells me that he, too, has been on several pilgrimages.

In this moment I see Brother Max in front of me and recognize his inner being. He speaks to me as a loving brother, one pilgrim to another; he knows what it means to be on the road. Now I can see why he had been so insistent in ensuring sleeping places for me. A pilgrim needs to know that at the end of a day he can put his weary head upon a pillow. The bottle of water in my room was put there in the knowledge that there is nothing more important for the wanderer than a good supply of fresh water. The small sweet is meant to be a special treat that cannot be expected every day; but today, dear pilgrim, somebody thought especially of you and wanted to bring you a little joy. The Easter decoration was important, too, because the pilgrim might not have been able to celebrate Easter properly on the road, or may have even forgotten about it altogether, having been on the road such a long time, just like Parzival on his journey.

Thus I hear Brother Max speak to me without words, and this language reaches deeply into my heart. And yet he is not what one might call a 'holy man'. He is a man in his prime, as one says, good-looking, with a healthy complexion and a joyful demeanour. Yes, we certainly share some hearty laughter! It is most probable that we will never see each other again, but this encounter truly 'touched' me and it is one of the most precious gifts of my journey.

It is also good to take leave now; after all, I have no wish to live in a monastery! I need to continue on my way. I walk out of the monastery very differently to how I entered it. Brother Max has extended his blessings to me. Ahead of me are the highest hills of my entire journey, and I have been given wings that carry me over these hills with inner joy and bliss at having met this human being! There is a song on my lips and a prayer in my heart!

My next lodgings are in Poppenhausen, one of the two places Brother Max arranged for me. On the way I climb one of the high hills called the Maulkuppe, and now I am deep in the heart of the Rhone, the land of my ancestors on my father's side. It is a landscape with alternating open meadows and woodland. It is a relief after the endless, dark forests through which I have travelled, and now snow-covered, open hills invite me. I am looking forward to the climb! I feel as if my soul is taking flight!

In Poppenhausen the nuns are expecting me. The mood in the nunnery is a good deal more sedate and serious than the monastery, even a little intimidating. The bed is hard, but clean. The food is somewhat bland and plain, and the nuns seem to hurry about, not stopping to speak with a stranger. My tired limbs, however, are so grateful for the bed, and I think of Brother Max who has arranged it all. I do not know where I would have been without his help! At breakfast-time Sister Saleria does come to sit with me for a little while, and gives me her blessing for the further journey.

The next day starts with sleet and continues with sleet as I climb the highest mountain of the Rhone, the Kreuzberg (Mount of the Cross). Full of reverence, I approach the monastery supposedly on its summit. The sleet turns into a blizzard and I am mightily glad when I see a large inn ahead of me. Inside it is crowded with people, laughing and shouting in front of their huge beer mugs. I ask one of them the way to the monastery and he looks at me sideways, exclaiming: 'This is the monastery, you are right in it!' And indeed, as I look around I can spot quite a few monks in the crowd. This monastery, as I later learn, is famed for its brewery, with its secret recipes dating back to the Middle Ages! Many people make long pilgrimages to sample the special brew! Staying the night here is just like an ordinary bed-and-breakfast, except for a notice in the room informing guests to observe reverent silence after 10 p.m. due to the sacred nature of this place. I am glad of it as I am exhausted from a strenuous day, and I want to be up early. But it is well after midnight before silence settles here, so I toss and turn for many an hour. Did Brother Max know where he had sent me? The monastery belongs to the same order of the Benedicts, and I would have thought they all know each other. Well, I now know Brother Max is a worldly soul! He must have been here many times on pilgrimage and joined in with the merry crowd! He really did think of everything!

Beyond the Iron Curtain

My next stop is with relatives on the eastern slopes of the Rhone. Here I also cross the former Iron Curtain. It is springtime and as I am walking due east it seems to keep pace with me, so that I have an experience—almost—of eternal spring. The blossoms on the fruit trees stay perfect for a good long month. This is a time of year I especially love. I often think that if I were told my time on earth was up I would plead to see and savour just one more Maytime, after which I would be ready to leave this beautiful earth.

The Rhone is a place to rest for a while. I have quite a number of close relatives here, among them my dear god-mother Melanie who shares my love of walking and is herself still going on walking holidays whenever her busy life allows her. She is in her early 70s and strides out beside me like a woman half her age as we go on a couple of day walks together.

As children we spent many summer holidays in this area. At that time it was still under Communist rule, and I can remember very clearly how the very air seemed different when we crossed that border coming from the West and encountered a very different culture. Both my parents came from East Germany originally but fled to the West while it was still just about possible. Later on, though with some difficulty, they visited their parents and siblings; but for a long time our East German relatives were not allowed to visit the West. My father in particular always felt very homesick for his little village and we went visiting practically every summer. Now I find my route has led me across the former border, which used to be called the 'death strip' as it was riddled with land mines. In some places memorial plaques commemorate those who tried to flee and lost their lives. Other parts of the former border have now turned into a nature reserve as a result of it being a 'no-go area' for so long. Nature has taken charge and let rare plants grow, providing a little paradise for the animal world. Later on I meet people who made it their task to turn the former 'death strip' into a 'life strip'.

The Rhone itself was cut in half by the Iron Curtain. This caused my father the greatest pain. As a schoolboy he could easily walk on foot to the village where his best friend lived, but after the war that village belonged to the West, and his to the East, and you then needed at least a whole day to get from one village to the other. The border was fiercely guarded by bad-tempered, unfriendly soldiers who ordered you about. Now this border has gone. In its place is a deep wound. The people from either side cannot understand one another even though they speak the same language. In the former eastern bloc, fear rules: the fear of being without work. Unemployment did not exist in communist times, neither did drug dealing, nor chain-stores. There were good provisions for working mothers, women had equal rights and opportunities, and pensions were secure—or so it seemed. All this has now changed. I meet many bitter people who see the riches of the West and feel marginalized. Some of them wish the days of communism would return, despite the repression that accompanied it. The people in the West, however, are fed up with having to listen to all these grumblings, and with pumping money into the former eastern bloc. Brothers and sisters no longer understand one another.

As a child I loved the Rhone area and identified myself with my father's deeply patriotic feelings. His childhood village still had a working smithy, and my great uncle was the smith. There was also a village bakery run by my father's cousin, who had lost one arm as a soldier in World War II. I admired the skill with which he placed the loaves of bread into the huge wood stove, then took them out again when they were done. Then the women would come with giant round baking trays balanced on their hips, filled with the local speciality of sweet flans, to be cooked in the slightly cooler oven after the bread had finished baking. The smell of this bakery was the very heart of my childhood! There was also a village tailor, another relative of mine—in other words, in those days it was a true village community. Now all of this has disappeared, bit by bit. I do, however, encounter one such idyllic scene on my walk, while accompanied by my godmother: we pass an old shepherd leaning on his staff, surrounded by his flock, musing in the sunshine. Spring is really here in all its glory with a beautiful early evening light; and silently, inwardly, I hear Beethoven's Pastorale as I perceive this luminous scene.

I take leave of my relatives and proceed eastwards. Again I feel as if I have crossed another threshold—beyond which my childhood memories don't reach—as I come ever closer to Germany's eastern borders.

Once again I walk through endless rain. The valley of the Werra is indeed very special with the local architecture of half-timbered houses, but I have very few addresses here and often I have to walk great distances in a day. I feel a tremendous loneliness and homelessness. I find myself sobbing from very deep within, and the feeling of homesickness seems to overpower me. At one point, yet again, I find myself without a place to sleep, and just as I resign myself to bedding down amongst the trees someone offers me their free-standing conservatory. I am in a town called Eisfeld ('Field of Ice') and that is exactly how it feels. The town is cold and reticent.

The next morning I visit the castle and find a plaque commemorating a torture practice that took place here. Apparently the methods of torture used were such that the victims became possessed by demonic beings; and on one occasion a human being was said to have changed into a werewolf, haunting the area as a wild beast until he was finally put to death. On reading this I shudder and hasten to leave.

The next day starts with rain, again, but as I climb up into the hills the clouds part and leave veils of mist in the valleys. I move as if through a painting by Caspar David Friedrich. I pass a spring with healing water (Itzquelle). Then I find my feet are wet and swollen and therefore decide to stop sooner than anticipated and book myself into a private bed-and-breakfast. This is where I meet a doll maker from the Ore Mountains and her poodle dog. She insists on hearing my whole story, and I have to promise to stop at her house when I get to the Ore Mountains. She has a friend in this village who is also a doll maker, and who fashions dolls according to photographs of children; we go to visit her. She used to work in a toy factory in communist times, and subsequently lost her job after unification. Thereupon she decided to start her own business and to work from home, and slowly developed her own 'speciality'. In time she became quite well known and has customers from all over the world. I found that it was often the women who took such courageous initiatives, whereas many of the men just hung around and talked about the good old days.

I meet another of these enterprising women in Sonneberg a few days later. She runs the local shop, and as I enter I see her surrounded by a whole bunch of men who seem to have nothing else to do. She asks me where I have come from and where I'm going, and then she exclaims, turning to the men: 'Do you hear that? This woman has walked all the way from England? Deserves a cup of coffee, I'd say!' She promptly disappears into her kitchen and returns with a steaming mug of coffee and a huge smile on her face! The men stare at me as if I had come from a different planet. This brave woman's encouragement spurs me on as I continue on my way.

At last the sun comes out again. In the villages I see beautiful Easter crowns decorating the wells, an old custom revived some ten years ago. I continue over open fields and meadows fragrant with flowers and edged with hedges in their young spring green. Thus I reach the romantic castle of Mitwitz, and from there scale the heights once more.

Today is the first of May. I bask in the sunlight and rejoice at the new growth in the trees, the blossoms, and the friendly white clouds. Many people are out walking today, spreading out into nature, and I am reminded of the Easter scene in Goethe's *Faust* describing the people leaving the prison of winter behind. I walk as if in a dream. A group of walkers invite me for a drink in the pub to celebrate the fact that I have walked here all the way from England!

The Power of Destiny

I am now approaching the Wernstein community, but the actual village is not on my route. I am, therefore, picked up by Erna, who lives in the community and who wrote to me before my departure to invite me to come. Erna and her husband are both artists, and parents of four boisterous boys. Life is not easy for them just now. The combination of being artists, parenting and sharing studio space seems difficult. Erna creates a lovely evening with an Indian meal and invites two other guests. We look at the walking maps and work out that I can do my next three sections whilst staying the nights in Wernstein, because people from the community are going out for work in different places and can pick me up at the end of the day and take me back again the next morning. In this way I can get to know the community a little. The room I am given is in a beautiful old house right opposite the splendid castle, and I can watch a sunset with blood-red colours from my window, with the silhouette of flowering fruit trees in front of the gates.

Erna takes me back to my path the next day. I find myself walking through one of the most beautiful stretches of my journey so far, along a valley and past old mill buildings, the spring sunshine accompanied by a fresh easterly breeze. At the end of the day I am picked up by her husband, Bernhard. During both car journeys I hear quite a few stories of their biographies, and the pain of both enters my soul. I recognize the struggle of contemporary marriage, with questions that people of former times did not have to wrestle with in quite the same way. And it is not easy to find out what destiny is asking of one. How can two such different people find a common path? My pilgrim's journey is like a metaphor of life itself. I take a certain decision and by doing so exclude other possibilities and opportunities. The path itself has an identity in its own right: after choosing one I find myself wondering how the other path has fared in the meantime. I take a decision in life to walk part of the way with a companion and by doing so exclude other possible companions. The question of freedom arises. There is the moment of meeting or decision-making, a very short fraction of time, and from there we must live through the consequences of that decision.

In the evening I meet one of the community's founder members, Reinhold Engel, and we go for a walk together. He tells me about the pioneer years in the '60s when the community came about at the invitation of the lord of the castle, who had the first biodynamic farm in the country. Later on, however, he renounced that way of life, and finding himself with huge debts finally had to sell the castle. Therefore it no longer belongs to the community.

Dusk falls whilst we walk and speak together. Then Reinhold takes me into an old and hidden cemetery in the woods, filled with a strange atmosphere. It has a tall, wrought iron fence all around it and the fence-poles create strange shadows and patterns in the evening light. Now I stand in front of the grave of Carl Alexander Mier, who was one of the founder members of the Biodynamic Agricultural Association and an early member of the Camphill movement (for people with special needs). Reinhold tells me that Carl came to see the Wernstein Community on his way to Bohemia,

where he intended to visit Karlstein Castle, the final destination of my own journey! But he died here quite suddenly
and so never got there. I feel my heart contract upon hearing
this strange story. Now I am very close to the Czech border,
which seems to me like a threshold to another world, and my
journey's goal is still somewhere in the blue distance. I, too,
cannot know at this point whether it will be granted to me to
reach my goal. I find myself deeply touched by the story of
this fellow traveller.

And this special day is not yet done. After the walk and
conversation with Reinhold I am invited to join a special
festival meeting of the community. The theme of the evening
is Whitsun, which is soon to be celebrated. A Christian
Community priest joins the meeting.

This priest used to live and work in the former Communist
part of Germany. The Christian Community was allowed to
exist under Communist rule with certain restrictions and, of
course, no support whatsoever from the government.

Tonight he speaks about the riddle of human destiny. To
meet our own individual destiny, he says, we need the other—
we cannot experience it in isolation. This sounds like a
paradox, and yet spiritual matters often appear as a paradox
to our earthly thinking, and we need to try to endure the
tension thereby created. Community living is an image of the
Whitsun event. At the end of the evening he gives a summary
of his talk in the form of a study he has worked with over
many years, which gives an overall context for the major
Christian festivals of the year.[9]

I leave the community again a few days later with all these
treasures in my heart. My route takes me from Nordhalben to
Schwarzenbad am Wald. My path leads me through dense,

dark woodland, totally secluded, amidst steep valleys of solitude. Today is quite a hot day and so I enjoy the coolness of the woodland. At midday I reach the fountain of Max-Marie and can refresh myself to my heart's content. What beautiful coincidence that the name of this water is the same as the monk who had refreshed my spirits! The voice of the forest speaks to me today in clear language. I respond by offering the Foundation Stone Meditation, speaking it aloud to the venerable old trees. I focus my senses to receive the impressions of this stretch of nature as purely as possible, listening to the melody of the wind in the foliage and feeling wrapped within it; I hear the birds singing, and the lively noise of the water that seems to seep out of every nook and cranny, bringing the gift of life itself.

In Schwarzenbach, Ursula and her mother pick me up. Ursula is a student of art therapy in Weimar, and I have been invited to visit and give a talk there. On the way the two of them show me the famous 'Well of Hell' (Höllenquelle), where carbonated water comes straight out of the ground. It flows continuously from the womb of the earth itself. Ursula also takes me to a 'ghost-town' (Hirschberg), which used to be just across the border behind the Iron Curtain, brutally dividing its people from the surrounding area. The tragedy of this period is illustrated by a terrible story told to me by Ursula. On the last day of World War II, the bridge spanning the steep valley leading to Hirschberg was destroyed by dynamite. Two people on a mission to carry messages on their motor bikes did not know this had happened and drove off the bridge, at full speed, into the deep gorge below. A woman in the town heard their terrible last cries as they tumbled down, and was never able to forget them. She ended her days in a mental hospital.

I listen to this story as we climb to the castle on the hill in the grey dusk. The castle no longer shows its former splendour and is now divided into cheap flats, completely neglected and uncared for. I cannot suppress my curiosity, and persuade Ursula to sneak inside and climb the mighty staircase in the hallway. The wallpaper has peeled away from the damp walls, and the spiralling staircase is covered in dirt, yet people do live here. But we don't meet anybody, either in the castle or in the streets of the town. Many windows of the houses have been covered with chipboard, and there seem to be hardly any shops selling anything. We turn to walk back in the moonlight.

The next day I am taken on a long car journey to visit the art therapy school in Weimar. They have heard about my journey, and that I am course director of a similar training in England, and want me to speak to the students.

I am warmly received and, after attending a couple of their lessons, I am invited to give my talk. It feels very strange for me to sit amongst colleagues. I feel a yawning gap between myself and my former life, so I cannot easily enter into the spirit of it. One of the tutors invites me to dinner, and she helps me come to terms with some of these contradictory feelings. Afterwards I have time to look around Weimar, this famous city of German culture which I also know from my childhood. Here, like everywhere else, they try to make the best of the huge political changes that have taken place, and you can still see remnants of the former Communist regime, side-by-side with the trappings of western consumer society.

In the evening I make a careful study of my walking maps. Soon I will have to decide which route to take: either following in Goethe's footsteps and crossing the border from the west via Karlsbad, Marienbad and Franzbad, on my way to

Prague, or skirting the German border and following it further north-east to visit Dresden, from where I would walk due south along the River Elbe.

That night I enter the following words in my diary: *Destiny, you are a silent goddess, veiled and hidden; you let me take my decisions in freedom and yet I cannot escape your embrace. And in the end you transform into future reality what I gain from my decision. I bow before you.*

Now I feel how very far away I am from home, from my former life. I no longer have firm roots in the ground. Something in me continues to shrink, something else is steadily growing. I don't yet know what it means. I can only feel my way forward, rather like walking in the darkness of a ghost-town. My former identity rooted in my work and family has completely fallen away from me. This is what I experience while giving my talk to the art therapy students in Weimar. I am not a teacher any more. I take my seat among them; I suffer with them. I listen to many stories of the life journeys that have brought this group together. Most of these students have grown up and lived in communist Germany, while most of their tutors are from the West. I listen; it is one station on my way, but I cannot linger long. I have to get up and meet what is coming towards me from the future.

That night I can finally make a decision. I opt for the considerable detour and visit the city of Dresden. It seems that I still hesitate to cross the border into the Czech Republic and that I need to explore Germany further east where I have not been before. The experience of the country of my birth has been greatly enriched by crossing it through its horizontal centre from the westernmost corner to here. I find out that there is a strip of East Germany with an ethnic minority called the Sorben, who, like the Welsh and Irish in Britain, speak an entirely different language, of Slavonic type. I feel drawn to this part of Germany, which looks so much poorer and yet so much more alive and full of potential.

In the meantime there has been a severe change in the weather. The temperature has dropped to 4°C, unheard of in May, and I have to meet this fact of life as I journey onwards. A dull and misty day receives me. Again I walk through deep woodland, and am greeted by a very special concert of bird-song, defying the cold, full of melody and rhythm such as I can't recall ever having heard before. The landscape is swathed in a strange and foreign atmosphere, dreamy and enchanted.

When after a couple of days the sun warms me again, I chance upon real little gems: a church in a village called Pilgrim, which seems an appropriate enough name for me to linger. I don't have a long way to walk today, so I decide to stay a while at lunchtime, and make myself at home in the churchyard.

I find a nice bench, from which I can admire the white-washed church decorated with reddish-brown cornerstones and an onion tower. Here I sit and read Victor Frankl's autobiography. I picture sitting in my own back garden enjoying some leisure time. Next to me is my own little cottage; any time I like I can go inside its walls and cook myself a meal, invite friends to dinner, go into my cosy bedroom to sleep. I imagine that many homeless people live in such a fantasy world. When our children were little they loved to hear a story of a poor Irish woman who always looked after other people's houses, never being in any that she could call her own. She was the servant, the nanny, the midwife, the cook for other people, wherever she was needed, forever moving on. And right at the end of her useful life she became homeless and still harboured a wish to have her own cottage to furnish to her own liking. The fairy folk listened to her keening and granted her wish, leading her to her own wee place that could be her own. And there she still dwells, inviting all those to come to her whose hearts are full of pain and sorrow, to find comfort and healing in her hospitality.

This dream of one's own home is shared even by nomadic people. The tent of the nomads, the wagon of the gypsies, is always beautifully decorated and furnished with the little things that make life homely and worth living. Everyday objects are lovingly decorated, painted, embroidered, woven in colours, fashioned by hand in wood or stone into little works of art. Today we live in a trash culture where things are often mass-produced, only to be discarded after use. Beauty no longer plays much part—utility is everything. Thus ugliness has arrived in our everyday world. This is what I experienced during my visit to the Sinai desert, where the Bedouin have been forced both by the government and by environmental changes to alter their sense of 'home', to live in corrugated, iron-roofed huts on the edge of the desert so that they can 'settle down' and be counted in numbers, thus fitting into the social order. Their indigenous culture is fast disappearing and now they live in poverty. Before, as nomads, they also had nothing, but they were not poor. They had everything they needed to live and more: beauty and art—the messengers of a higher world with the power to transform our existence on earth into true living. The new poverty of our time is harsh and relentless, soul-destroying and unbearable. Devoid of humanity, our urban environments attract criminality and destructiveness.

Accompanied by these thoughts I read Victor Frankl's account of life in a concentration camp, an environment dehumanized in the extreme, and even the last vestige of human dignity extinguished. Here ugliness became a tool to subordinate people to the evil power of manipulation, death and destruction. It is deeply moving to read how, when the soul has been stripped bare of everything and there is nothing left at all but oneself, one still has a choice: to succumb or grow into infinity. A terrible battle for the survival of the soul is fought in the context of unspeakable horror, in the abyss of humanity, a battle whose outcome matters to us all and our possibilities for future development.

Eventually I have to leave my dreaming and pondering place and take to the road again. All these accumulated thoughts and feelings come with me, waiting to find expression somehow, somewhere ...

The next few days take me to the Czech border, where I symbolically place one foot across the divide. But honouring my decision to take the north-eastern path I stay in Germany itself, nevertheless crossing the former border of the Iron Curtain several times. At one such, now invisible border crossing I find a plaque with the names of people who lost their lives trying to flee to the West.

Both the capitalist and the communist systems have bred a great deal of ugliness in their time. Now that the Iron Curtain has gone there are still remnants of the farming practices of that time. My path leads me through woodland and also open fields with vast stretches of monoculture, the result of communal farming under the Communist regime where environmental issues were brushed aside in favour of big yields, and different farms were forced to compete with one another. Any hedges have long been rooted out; there are only rectangular parcels of land, and the corresponding feeling is one of emptiness and desolation.

Today I walk some 35 kilometres and arrive totally exhausted in Kottengrün. The house I am staying in proves to be something of a little oasis. The artistic and ecologically minded family has lovingly renovated it. Both the parents work actively for the regeneration of the landscape that has suffered so much. They are such positive and joyful people and it is a real pleasure to meet them. They live their daily life with great creativity and enthusiasm, and their enthusiasm is infectious.

I find myself next in the Vogtland, which is a part of Germany I had never even heard of before receiving a lovely letter from Rosie, who read about my pilgrimage and got in touch to invite me to stay with her family. Just prior to my departure she sent another letter of encouragement. This gives me the feeling that we know each other a little already. She wrote to me enthusiastically about this region—a place steeped in history, situated between the Frankenwald and the Ore Mountains, and with quite a few castles, many with a strong link to Karl IV.

Rosie and I meet at the bottom of a wooded valley: all of a sudden she appears to me out of the trees, a small yet strong woman whose eyes sparkle, and whose soft voice speaks a hearty welcome. We are both overjoyed to meet like this!

She invites me to spend a little time in Jocketa, her home town. I learn many things about this particular area and also about the vast forests that I have already travelled through. Rosie's husband is a fund of geographical knowledge. He shows me that the Frankenwald is really the very heart of

Europe, whereas the Fichtelgebirge (Fichtel Mountains) form the centre of a cross. I can feel how I am coming nearer and nearer to what I long to find. I finally lose my fear of the unknown. Now I feel strong enough to cross the borders without hesitation and to open myself to the new. It feels good to be here.

Rosie takes me to the amazing red brick viaducts for which the Vogtland is famous. There are two of them, and one is the largest in the world. When it was built in 1841 over 30 people suffered fatal accidents during its construction. Even today it acts like a magnet for the death wishes of desperate people who come here to end their lives. The Göltschtal bridge stands as a mighty relic of the Industrial Revolution in this part of Germany, a pioneering feat of engineering of its time.

The Ore Mountains

After a heartfelt celebration I take my leave of the family. It is difficult to get going again after these days of 'home life'. I cross through the remainder of the Vogtland and find myself in woodland again. At some point I feel a total change of mood in the landscape and I realize that I have entered the Ore Mountains! Outwardly there is no real difference and yet it is quite clear that I have crossed an invisible boundary. A deeply melancholic mood lies over the land here.

Now the woodland becomes denser and darker and I feel that it harbours many secrets. Every now and then I see the remnants of the mining activity that gives this stretch its character and name. Even the humble gravel stones on the paths glitter like gemstones in the sunlight and I feel as if in the land of hidden treasures.

It wasn't until the twelfth century that this area of Germany first became inhabited. Before that time it would have been an untouched wilderness of virgin forest. One day somebody discovered a vein of silver in the rock and from then on the signature of human activity changed this landscape and the woodlands forever. Much richness and wealth issued from this land until, with the exhaustion of the silver mines, this met a sudden end. The people were plunged into poverty and destitution, and could no longer find a livelihood. Then, somewhere else, another vein of precious ore was discovered; people crowded in and built a new settlement, until one day these riches came to an end too.

The Ore Mountains harbour forces of light and dark in close proximity. Its people are devout and even today honour the turns of fortune that destiny brings. Nowhere else have I seen more beautiful village churches, imbued with a mood of devotion, originating from the profound depths of the human soul and from an immediate recognition of the divine in earthly life. The menfolk spent most of their daylight hours in the bowels of the earth, hardly ever seeing the sun, but becoming acquainted with the mysteries of the interior of the earth, the dwelling place of Tubal Cain.[10] This experience produced a particularly devotional relationship to the forces of the light. Their women brought lanterns to the entrance of the mine-shafts at Christmastime, so that the men could perceive the light upon their return, at night, from the depths. The men regarded their women as angels. When a boy child was born they placed a hand-carved figure of a miner in the window because his destiny was already pre-determined, but when the newborn was a girl they placed a wooden angel. Today these wooden symbols are sold all over the world as Christmas decorations, but few people are aware of their connection with the daily life of the people of the Ore Mountains.

In times of poverty it was the women who took the initiative, and whose skills saved lives. It is said that one of them invented the specific type of lace-making that you still find in this area. There is a statue to honour her memory in Annaberg-Buchholz. The men, when they found themselves unemployed, took to wood carving and fashioned those symbols of their existence: the figure of the miner as a nut-cracker; the angel; the pyramid with the candles, which is an image of the mechanism that transported the miners into their shafts; and also the little Christ-child figure in the cradle, who placed the light inside human hearts. Nowhere else in the whole world do they celebrate Christmas as they do here, and even two generations of communism could not alter this. Thousands of candles, I was told, are lit throughout the Holy Nights, in the churches and in remote cottages in the deep woods, which stand silent in their thick covering of snow. Sacred music and carols are also heard in these remote corners.

Now I am approaching the town of Schneeberg, which I reach at the end of a long and weary day of walking, some 40 kilometres. I have walked for many hours through the darkness of these woods and now at last I see the town in the distance, with its prominent church perched on the very top of the hill like a mother hen lovingly protecting its chicks. As I come nearer I see how impressive it is, full of decorative carvings crafted by skilled hands. I feel unable to walk another step. I am spent.

Often on this journey I have marvelled at the restorative powers of sleep! Once again, it works its magic—I wake in the morning and feel ready for anything! The first thing I do is visit the church properly. I find out that it was almost totally destroyed in World War II and then rebuilt, painstakingly, stone by stone. The interior was left utterly simple, stunningly beautiful. It houses a most important treasure, a triptych from the sixteenth century from the workshop of Lucas Cranach the Elder.

The other end of town, however, has been marred by the brutal architecture of the communist era. There is nothing graceful or beautiful in these high-rise blocks, no joy in the endless repetition of uniformity. However, the people are wonderfully friendly and now and then someone stops to talk with me. I find it interesting that people do not respond to my remarks about the landscape's incredible beauty, as if they have only ever related to its usefulness or hostility in times of hardship.

Today is 17 May and I find out that my friend Rosemary—who was at my farewell party and gave me the necklace of freshwater pearls—has died. On my further journey I enter the church of Schlettau, one of the oldest settlements in the Ore Mountains, and here in the stillness of its interior I think of her further journey. My soul feels raw and open, and that is why I can feel her very close to me. I talk to her, describe to her all that has touched me on this pilgrimage, particularly my most recent experiences of these mountains. I show her the special altar of this church, a piece of folk art with lots of bright colours in a carved frame, reminiscent of some far-eastern sacred art. In the silence I find myself weeping for all the pain in the world, mourning her passing. Her story showed me the transformative power of pain, like the grain of sand in the oyster which turns to pearl.

In the meantime I have arrived at the doll-maker's house. She is very eager to receive me and wants to show me as much as possible of the Ore Mountains. She drives me to many places and we can only look at things very briefly before we move on to fit everything in. I am completely swamped by all these impressions and can hardly remember any of it. At the end she proudly shows me the doll museum, which she founded, where you can find dolls of all descriptions, from elaborate nineteenth-century beauties to distorted, twenty-first-century plastic creations. I thank her for the effort she put into the sightseeing, which gave me the opportunity to see places I would not otherwise have been able to visit. Yet I have to admit to myself that sightseeing itself is really no longer meaningful to me.

On the way back we stop once more to look at a particularly beautiful village church in Großrückerswalde. It is fashioned entirely of wood, and served its people not only as a house of God but also as a refuge in times of war and famine. Its eaves were used as a grain store during days of hardship, and the balconies served as watchtowers to spy an approaching enemy. I see a poster announcing a concert in the church next day. As I have decided to stop for an extra day of rest, I have time to go to the concert, which turns out to be a most uplifting experience in this amazing venue decorated with simple folk art, which blends most beautifully with the sound of the instruments.

That evening I listen to yet another story of these mountains—this time a more contemporary one—told by the doll-maker's husband. After World War II, uranium was discovered in these rocks, for use in the nuclear industry. Once again the men went down into the bowels of the earth, many of them conscripted. No one told them about the need for protection from radiation, and many a strong man suffered a premature, painful death as a result, adding their numbers to the victims of this terrible and beautiful landscape.

When I finally take my leave on the third day, I discover another treasure—the church of Wiesa, built in the style of the Arts and Crafts movement of the nineteenth century. Outside it is not so different in shape from the traditional Ore Mountain churches: a square base with an attractive onion-shaped tower in the middle. The interior, however, is a gem, richly decked out with colours that have been carefully chosen to harmonize with each other, and present a glorious and festive space.

I sit in the front row near the altar and let all the impressions work upon me. I see a group of young people rehearsing a play that tells the story of the woman of Samaria. She is the one who meets the Christ, and whose deeper being he recognizes; he also points to her dark side. Yet the Christ speaks his words in love and forgiveness and so they do not wound, but heal. She can pick up the thread of her life again and know the inner joy that comes from meeting one's destiny.

There is one more church I need to mention, which lies in Lauterbach. Again it is very ancient, and has served as a fortress in times of need. In the little churchyard I find a perfect resting place to eat my noontime bread, just as a small funeral procession winds its way past the graves accompanied by a sombre brass band. A much larger parish church was built in the seventeenth century, and so the church itself was shifted, bit by bit, from its original site in the middle of the village to just outside it, in the fields. It now serves as a funeral chapel, and I imagine that the people of this village still prefer its quiet, humble shape with the old woodwork and primitive paintings to the grander, more imposing church, and long to have their final resting place in its protective shade.

In the afternoon I reach the town of Zöblitz where I have to ask an older woman for directions. After she describes the way she obviously wants to continue talking to me and ends up telling me quite a lot of her life story. Originally she hailed from the Baltic and came to this area as a refugee after the war. Does she miss the sea? She replies: 'Oh, as long as there is woodland I am happy. The wood is as beautiful as the sea!' I am touched by this meeting, as normally two strangers passing one another in the street would not end up telling their biography. It has happened before on this pilgrimage, and I am wondering whether the fact that I will be walking on, and we will most likely not meet again, enables people to share their deeper feelings.

Now I continue on my path through the woods along a silvery, bubbling brook to the village of Obernhaus, where I treat myself to a warm dinner of fried potatoes with onion. There is nowhere for me to stay and I have to travel further. A nice man on a bicycle comes with me for part of the way to make sure I don't get lost as dusk is falling. I climb steeply until I reach the edge of the woods, and then come out into a wide-open space just in time to see the last glow of the sunset. Here in the little hamlet of Heidendorf I am lucky enough to find a bed with a nice family on a smallholding, who cannot hear enough about my story.

On this stretch of my journey I find myself working through a lot of issues in my biography. Through the rhythm of walking I am led again and again into my inner landscape, and I see that a lot of work still needs to be done. I, too, know a dark side of myself like the biblical woman of Samaria. Inasmuch as I am able to truly forgive myself, I find strength to forgive others. But it has to start with myself, this is what counts. It is the most important step and one that enables me to get close to the love of Christ, the love that the woman of Samaria was blessed enough to experience.

It is now that I work particularly with the second verse of the Foundation Stone Meditation:

Human Soul!
You live in the beat of heart and lung
Which leads you through the rhythm of time
Into the realm of your own soul's feeling.
Practise *spirit presence*
In soul composure,
Where the weaving deeds
Of universal becoming
Unite
The individual I
With the I of the World;
And you will truly *feel*
In the active life of your soul.

Then the answer:

For the Christ Will is present all around
In world rhythms shedding grace on our souls;
Spirits of Light!
May what is formed by the west
Have been quickened in the light of the east;

This part of the meditation has now become reality for me and
has become part of me. Rosemary accompanies me further:

Proclaiming:
In Christ death becomes life.
The elemental spirits hear it
In east, west, north, south:
*May hu*man beings *hear it!*

The following night, by what seems like strange coincidence, I
find myself sleeping beneath the portraits of Ulbricht,[11]

Honecker[12] and Hitler! My own shadow is connected to the shadow of humanity. It is the essence of esoteric Christianity, so strongly rejected by these three individuals and by the Churches, that Christ's forgiveness is there for all of us.

I leave the Ore Mountains, richly blessed on my inner journey, and I celebrate my departure in the secret garden of an enchanted château that I find just outside Dippoldswalde, near Dresden.

Dresden

I reach Dresden on Ascension day and decide to take a break from walking as I want to make the most of this famous city. I am glad to see a signpost pointing in the direction of Prague and telling me it is 135 kilometres away! So it is no longer far! I can hardly believe that I have journeyed all this way (135 km feels like hardly any distance now). I even feel a pang of sadness that my journey will be over soon.

As I have been so starved of cultural activities I draw deeply on the potential of this place. I go to hear a strangely beautiful concert of Bedouin music in the interior of the Church of Our Lady, which is in the process of reconstruction. I decide to buy myself a ticket to Verdi's opera *Jerusalem* in the famous Semper Opera House. It seems strange to arrive in these grand places with my walking gear, but of course there is no choice!

I go to see the *Sistine Madonna* by Raphael, which I have known from many reproductions. What a different experience it is to stand in front of the original, with all the subtleties that can never really be properly reproduced, and also to see it in its proper size! I also view the Rembrandt collection, and spend some time with the paintings of Caspar David Friedrich as a preparation for my journey ahead through Saxon Switzerland (Elbsandsteingebirge).

With my host family I visit the castle of Pillnitz the following day. This splendid building served as a pleasure castle for August the Strong, who was responsible for a multitude of splendid buildings in Dresden. And on the evening of the next day I am treated to a most wonderful open-air concert of classical music, complete with a glowing sunset over the river against the silhouette of the city—an unforgettable experience.

Altogether I spent the best part of a week in Dresden, staying in three different households. My first hosts are a group of young female students, one of whom has a little baby—who is passed around the whole group, so it takes me quite a while to work out who the mother is! We sit on the balcony in the evening light and I ask them about their upbringing in communist times and how they have adjusted to the new system. I am impressed by their insights and very mature assessment of this recent episode of history, as well as their freshness and joy in life.

My second hosts are a couple in their early thirties who have also just had a baby, and are still feeling a little insecure about being parents. Michael, the child's father, has an interesting job as a probation officer, specializing in bringing the perpetrators of crime face-to-face with their victims (restorative justice). In the past he worked as a planning officer in Dresden and therefore can point out the more hidden, interesting features of the city, and the more recent additions to its suburbs, where one can also still experience the kind of scenery reminiscent of a more rural time.

For the last couple of days I am the guest of an older couple whose children have long since left home. In my conversation with the husband, once an eminent scientist, it emerges that his very first memory was of the night of the Dresden bombing, when he was about three. He can talk about this event without any trace of bitterness and with deep understanding, as well as with great observation of detail, both in relation to the outer event and to what went on inside him.

Today we look on from a distance as war and senseless destruction bring untold suffering, poverty and desolation. We can afford to ignore it as it is not, at present, on our doorstep; we look on as families are torn apart, and helpless people are sent to their deaths in the most brutal manner, often suffering terrible torments. Priceless cultural sites and buildings are destroyed forever.

The people of Dresden decided after the war to leave their famous cathedral of Our Lady as a ruin. It became a shrine for peace, where people from all over Europe congregated once a year in a candlelit memorial ceremony to symbolize the common wish for peace. More recently the decision was taken to rebuild the cathedral; most of the other historical buildings having been restored to the former splendour of the time when Dresden was known as the second Venice of Europe. I do question the wisdom of this reconstruction, and wonder whether it might not have been better to keep this potent memorial of wartime destruction. Rebuilding it seems to devalue the suffering and loss endured by the people of Dresden, alongside many other cities, almost as if these events never happened.

I conclude my visit to Dresden by honouring one of the most outspoken critics of war, the artist Käthe Kollwitz, who towards the end of a long life full of suffering and loss lived near the castle of Moritzburg (a suburb of Dresden). The castle itself is beautiful, surrounded by water mirroring light; and yet it seems strangely empty and devoid of meaning, having served the pleasures of the wealthy of its day. Now it is just a honeypot for tourists. Near the castle is a museum of

Kollwitz's striking graphic work, showing the faces of human beings distorted by unspeakable pain, mothers who lose their children because they can no longer feed them, others who look for their dead sons on battlefields. Sometime she depicts the figure of Death himself as he tears the mother away from her starving child; or there is a mother who holds her dead son over her lap like a modern day *pietà*. 'Never again war!' is written all over one of her drawings, which served as a poster for the anti-war movement.

My first encounter with Käthe Kollwitz's work was in the westernmost part of Belgium—near the battlefields where she lost both her son and later her grandson in the two World Wars. Here, in this prominent corner of Eastern Germany where she died, in the building now dedicated to her memory, I close this circle. In between lie all the intersecting paths of the destiny of Central Europe, a destiny that was altered forever by the events of those wars and still bears the scars.

The destiny of Dresden poses many questions: about the destiny of the German nation as a whole in relation to each individual human being within it; and about the destiny of the whole of Europe during the most recent events that have unfolded here. These questions are reflected in this most fascinating city, that is now struggling to shake off the memories of its terrible past so that it can step forward to take its place in the twenty-first century.

Elbsandsteingebirge

The next leg of my journey takes me through the Elbsand-steingebirge, also known as 'Saxon Switzerland', which various people have now told me about. I have also of course seen the paintings of Caspar David Friedrich in Dresden, as well as the fine drawings of Ludwig Richter. The landscape was a favourite subject of the Romantic period. I am looking forward to it very much.

From Dresden the footpath largely follows the river Elbe, which makes it quite easy and straightforward except for the occasional sudden diversions onto busy main roads and through ugly industrial estates (just as I remembered from my time in Flanders). My other obstacle is a strong northwesterly wind that decides to put up a fight with me, as I walk along listening to the sound it makes in the trees. So it is a very windswept, scraggy figure that arrives in the town of Pirna. Here two lady hosts receive me, and take it in turns to look after me and introduce me to their many friends. They are full of amazement that a woman from England has walked all the way to their humble little town. In the end I am even taken to the press, who take my picture and interview me for the local paper.

I am truly amazed by this place. The old part is really quite splendid despite still bearing the marks of years of neglect under the communists, but restoration work is in full swing, beginning with bringing some colour back onto the buildings' exteriors. Paint, I am told, was only sold in shades of grey in communist times. Going a bit further back to Nazi times, the old castle acquired notoriety as a mental hospital where patients became research objects for medical experiments, often resulting in death or lifelong disfigurement. Now it has been put up for tender and had just been acquired by an American firm that wants to convert it into a luxury hotel. What a change of fortune, but I ask myself: what spirit will now prevail here?

Back with my hosts I meet somebody who served in the army as a high-ranking officer under the communists and carried out his duties with full inner conviction and idealism. With the fall of that regime his whole worldview collapsed, throwing him into a deep inner crisis. Some people in his position actually committed suicide, unable to bear looking at the abyss that opened up in them when all they had worked for, believed in, and given their heart's blood to, was suddenly exposed as corrupt and full of lies. He speaks about his experiences, full of humility, not hiding the pain that has accompanied this process. Facing his own vulnerability he managed to transform his idealism, remaining true to it with inner conviction. He is now working in an old people's home, bringing to it his full commitment, humanity and capacity for empathy, and alleviating their daily routine with special artistic programmes that he designs.

My next destination is Königstein, where I am due to take a ferry to the other side of the river and continue along its banks for a little while longer. I come to a bend of the river and find myself making a great entrance into the strange landscape of the Elbsandsteingebirge. Suddenly I see tower upon tower of basalt rock, growing out of the landscape from nowhere, like a fossilized forest of giant remnants from a time when the earth still heaved with life. Even today these rock columns look like sleeping monsters that could awaken at any moment and wreak havoc. I climb high, which affords a stunning view deep down to the bend of the River Elbe where I was walking not that long ago. From here I can also see the strangely shaped hills of rock fortresses that rise up almost vertically from the river plane, and then dramatically angle off nearly horizontally at the top.

Until the end of the eighteenth century very few would have ventured into this forbidding landscape as it was too full of obstacles and dense forests to be of any agricultural use. It was the artists of the Romantic era who discovered the beauty in this bizarre handiwork of Mother Nature, and began to explore it—with great difficulty as there were no footpaths or other signs of human activity. They were well rewarded as they delved ever further into the interior, finding ever more dramatic natural sculptures. Today of course it is one of the most popular areas in eastern Germany and I encounter many tourists, which makes solitude impossible. With one of them I have a brief exchange, a lonely figure like myself who hails from England and returns year after year to walk in silent determination between these rocks.

Towards the end of the day I reach Lilienstein, one of these lonely rock plateaux, and I even experience a kind of vertigo standing at the top surrounded by nothing but air. Later on I hear a terrible story that took place here some 30 years ago. A group of schoolchildren were perched on the edge of the rock as it gave way, dragging many of them down into the depths. Their teacher, who watched horror-struck, jumped after them.

I can see how this landscape is full of magnetic fascination.

There is nothing soft and yielding about it, no flowing lines other than the impressive meandering of the river. It commands respect but does not let you rest. It sends shivers down your spine as you dare to step to the edge of an abyss of sucking darkness. The landscape invites you to cross your own boundaries, to dare the impossible. My host that evening is a passionate rock climber who scales the vertical walls, without ropes or any other equipment. But there is sweetness in the air as the scent of elderflowers envelops me—a wonderful contrast to the masculine energy of the rocks. This is the moment when I decide in my heart to write this book and paint these pictures, in an attempt to trace the inner journey that has engraved itself upon my soul. I know already that I will have to overcome many obstacles to do so, fighting for the space in my busy life to give this priority.

I am so close now to the end of my pilgrimage, and increasingly I feel the tremendous distance I have travelled from my former life as my thoughts begin to reach back again, knowing that sooner or later I will have to face up to it. It seems vital, therefore, to hold on to what has started to germinate within me and to pledge to honour it and give it its due. It is a similar pledge that I made to myself as a child: not to forget what it feels like to be a child no matter how old I become. With this journey I have been able to fulfil one of my life's deepest longings, but the fruit of it is not mine alone—it needs to be offered in the first instance to all those who have made it possible, and to give courage to those who themselves wish to explore their inner landscapes.

It is 1 June when I finally cross the border to the Czech Republic near Janov. I linger a bit on the way, in the town of Bad Schandau, before climbing up to the Schrammsteine, the most dramatic rock formation thus far. The weather has contributed to the mood by alternating brilliant hot sunshine with thunderstorms, producing strange light phenomena in the deep gullies that mingle with the colours of the summer vegetation. Looking into the vast distance, I feel as if transported into an embrace with eternity itself, bringing me to the boundary of physical reality, where time and space merge. I feel like praying, to give thanks for being allowed to fill myself with these thoughts and feelings. My pilgrimage has become divine celebration.

It is in this mood of inner communion that I now approach the long-awaited border to the Czech Republic, but I am rudely jolted out of it by the noise of the many stall keepers and purchasers lining the road, which is covered in dirt and trash. I cannot find a bed in Hrensko; everything is booked up. I am tired and it has started to rain again. I pace back and forth along the road, not able to make a decision as to what to do. Studying my map I spot a footpath along a small river leading to a settlement, and so I resolve to get there despite my tiredness. The path winds along a beautiful wild brook with sheer rock on either side creating a very narrow passage for its waters. After about 3 kilometres I suddenly find myself faced by iron gates that are firmly locked, and with no other passage. So there is nothing for it but to turn back again to Hrensko with all its ugliness. Dead tired, I creep up a hill along the main road to Janov, where I find the last available room, in a fairly grim and dirty place.

That night I have a dream as an echo to my thoughts of the previous day. It appears like a warning, telling me to stay true to my resolve. Upon waking I can just grasp hold of the theme of my biography that has led me to undertake this journey, and I see the different circles of my life interpenetrating: that of my birth family, my marriage and my own family, and my profession. The difficulties in each of the circles impact on one another and I recognize that I have to find new ways of resolving those difficulties.

Now I am in the Czech Republic, and the border is nothing like the huge threshold I imagined. The landscape continues with even more bizarre and dramatic formations. Many people are out walking as it is the Whitsun holiday weekend. I meet an older person who tells me that originally he came from this area when it still was part of Germany. After the war he and his family became refugees. Now they come here every year and have a family reunion.

My adventures with the Elbsandsteingebirge continue as I pass the Prebischtor and the Saunsteine, where I become quite daring in clambering up rocks with breathtaking views—before descending again, worried that I may not find accommodation. But that night I am lucky. I find a pretty wooden house in the traditional style, which is very unusual. It is called 'Umgebindehaus', meaning two houses one inside the other, with the outer one supported by pillars that are often decorated most elaborately with carvings and paintings. I find myself now in the dreamland of the Bohemia of my childhood, just as I imagined it then, full of fairy tale images and a mystical air conjured up by the richly coloured woods in a wild landscape. Houses that have been built so lovingly speak of the importance of a human dwelling place in a hostile land. Home becomes an oasis in the wilderness, promising comfort, the place to rest, eat and live. And because of this importance, the house is built with love and care and becomes a work of art, symbolizing also the need for nourishing and nurturing the inner life.

After lofty heights, on the next day, Whit Sunday, I enter a deep gorge formed by the forces of water, whose energies still echo in the wild brook. I pass ruined houses and caves, and come to Jetrichovice, a village full of colourful houses. Now I reach the end of the Elbsandsteingebirge and have to admit to a feeling of relief in finding peace again in the landscape after so much ruggedness (which has made demands on my inner life!). I welcome the break from drama to focus myself on this last stretch of my pilgrimage.

Towards Prague, the Golden City

Now the journey continues through a softly undulating landscape, with the distinctively shaped hills of Bohemia. The path winds through green meadows and fields, past occasional small orchards and colourful country cottages. I take a little rest in the garden of a pilgrim's chapel and contemplate the fact that it is Whitsun. Just at that moment I receive an unexpected phone call on my mobile phone from one of my hosts back in Belgium to wish me a happy Whitsun! It gladdens my heart to think that my journey is accompanied by the thoughts of other people. It is astonishing that these relatively brief meetings with my hosts along the way have created some substance between us. I can remember this particular lady very well—she was leading quite a lonely life, preoccupied by a search for meaning and healing, and suffering many pains along the way. She told me quite a bit of her biography, which touched me deeply. Her cottage was tucked away in a lonely rocky landscape with a wild brook meandering through it, not unlike the one I encountered on entering the Czech Republic. Again I think about all the bridges that a pilgrimage can build. And with this particular connection a bridge has been built between Belgium and Bohemia. Karl IV, the beloved King of Bohemia, had a father from Luxembourg and a mother from this part of the world; he spent his childhood in France and later settled for the rest of his life in Bohemia.

Yet soon I find my spirits at an all-time low. I am fighting my way through a continual drizzle of rain that by now seems to have lasted forever. My shoes are no longer watertight, although I am grateful that they have lasted this long. I feel a great need to rest. I am worried about falling ill. There are no addresses here of people I could stay with and when, in the end, I find myself in an ugly, run-down hotel with unfriendly people in Novy Bor, I decide that enough is enough, I have to do something. I do have a Servas address in Liberec, except that this town is not at all on my route. I decide to telephone them anyway to ask whether I can come. They sound so welcoming that I take a train journey there with the idea of returning to Novy Bor when I have recovered my strength again. My feet are completely softened by the waterlogged shoes and I can feel the start of blisters again, so it is time to act.

Throughout the train journey the rain seems to come down in buckets. I cannot look out of the windows as they are misted over. The compartment is absolutely packed. Opposite me is a woman who tries desperately to make contact with me by means of a little pocket dictionary and sign language. She no doubt wants to find out what I am about in my strange attire, obviously not being a teenage backpacker yet travelling with a big rucksack.

At the train station in Liberec my wonderful host picks me up—an elderly gentleman who takes me to a huge high-rise block, which in its heyday used to house some 3000 people. The gentleman and his lovely wife tell me their story: how they suffered as Catholics in Communist times. They both worked as professors at a university but had to give up this work under mounting pressure from party politics. He also tells me of the time when he went on a protest march with a

group of others, from Liberec to Prague, some 70 miles—
walking all through the night in one go! I am mightily
impressed!

Whilst in Liberec with this lovely couple I continue learning more valuable facts about the Czech people and their
history. They are both extremely knowledgeable and actively
engaged in contemporary issues. I hear how the Czech people
regard Karl IV as the benevolent father of their nation. Both
my hosts are amazed that I have this strong connection to
Karl IV, without being a Czech. They also tell me about the
unique form of resistance the Czechs put up against the
Communist regime imposed on their country. The majority of
people never really embraced communist ideals, devising
some unique methods of resistance. For example, if high-
ranking communist officials entered a restaurant, they would
be ignored for as long as possible—or until they decided
themselves that it was better to leave.

I am deeply grateful for this couple's wonderful hospitality.
I feel I learn so much from them, and have been given more
riches to guide my way. For the short time I stay in their flat
they give me a real home and make me feel so welcome. This
is in stark contrast to the fact that their flat is a tiny speck on a
massive block, bigger than any I have come across before.
When I look at it from outside, at the rows and rows of
windows and balconies, I can see how this form of architecture was designed to make the individual feel totally
insignificant. It is a tribute to the strength of the human spirit
that some, at least, succeeded in retaining and even developing their humanity under these circumstances.

The endless rows of blocks of flats remind me of an inner
death experience I had in my late teens. I was about 17 and

was in lodgings away from home for the first time. I was employed in a children's home as a student on work experience, yet I found myself as deeply unhappy as I had been in my parental home. One night I decided to go for a walk because the feelings of hopelessness and emptiness seemed overwhelming. I had to pass endless blocks of flats, favoured in West Germany also as a quick and cheap method of providing housing in the 60s. After the destruction of the war they seemed to mushroom out of the ground at the edges of towns and cities. In my inner despair this architecture became a metaphor for the unrelenting greyness of adult life, as I perceived it then. These rows of houses seemed to come closer and closer, suffocating me and sucking my last strength. All of a sudden a powerful resistance arose in me with the strength of a mighty natural force, such as an earthquake or a hurricane. My soul became one long cry of protest, and inwardly I screamed: 'Whatever happens, I will not let myself be robbed of what is most precious to me!' That very night I came to one of the most decisive decisions I have ever taken in my life: to turn my back on the path others had laid out for me, and to follow my own star. The next day, without telling anyone, I emptied my bank account of its meagre contents to get myself abroad. It proved to be the beginning of three desperate years of homelessness when I often found myself in danger or in the depths of inner desolation. Those were my dark years in the shadows, which only came to an end around the age of 20 or 21.

I often look back to this night-time walk between the blocks of flats and remind myself that in this one single moment I made a decision that profoundly affected my life and has been a guide to me ever since; it tells me that it is of the utmost importance to listen to this inner voice, regardless of the consequences for oneself, one's comfort and love of ease. Despite the difficulties and darkness that resulted from my decision, I know in my heart that I would have lost something extremely precious and important had I chosen to ignore that call. The decision was born out of a deep wound, and pain so deep that it is hard to put into words. I only knew one thing—that I needed to remain true to myself and to walk my path by this light only. I now think that it was my dead grandmother who stood by me through the times of trial and danger. She who told me the fairy tales gave me the gift of courage for my whole life, despite the fact that, like other people, I am really such a coward. Courage is the gift that we can truly give to each other. It is the other side of the coin of trusting one's destiny.

The experience of my youth is linked very closely to my pilgrimage. Now I find myself again homeless as I was then, and dependant on the good will of others; but this time it is a choice born of joy and the wish to celebrate. It is as if the shadows of my past can finally be resurrected and brought into the light. In this way I can feel how my journey is breaking the spell of an old enchantment and freeing me at last from the confusing and dark feelings of that time, which could so easily have sent me into the abyss of an unpredictable underworld.

My hosts offer to take me back to Novy Bor, from where I pick up my path again after taking fond leave of them, and walk to Ceska Lipa through the woods and among the rocks. At last I reach a very special spot that is a former hermitage, and I rest a while simply because it is filled with such a lovely mood. Later I come into the 'Valley of Hell' (Peklo), a swampy stretch of woodland with rare plants, edged by mighty rock formations. Journeying on from there I reach the village of Zahradnik. In this village I am supposed to find the holiday house of my friends in Prague, who eagerly await my arrival. They themselves will not be there but they have said I can pick up the key from the neighbours and make use of it. I thought the cottage would not be far from Zahradnik, but I could not have been more wrong! First of all I find myself thoroughly lost in the forest! Tired and exhausted I finally resolve to follow the tarmac road, after reproaching myself for still not being able to read the map properly. It is already well into the night when I find the house at last, after almost despairing—after all, how will anyone understand me? At last I meet the nice neighbour who speaks impeccable English and who had been told I am coming—so he has been on the look-out for me for quite some time. He shows me how to light a fire in the tiled stove. It is on top of this stove that I make my bed for the night, just as in fairy tales! The next day this helpful neighbour gives me good advice about the best route to take next. I walk through remote Bohemian villages that belong to a different era from ours. I can feel the end of my journey approaching. No one is astonished any more when they hear that I am on my way to Prague!

It is a dreamily beautiful landscape and the scent of summer is in the air. Today I feel as if in a cathedral as I walk through the woods. I speak the Foundation Stone Meditation out of the fullness of my heart, into the solitude of the forest, and there it is well received. I feel a response to it as it resonates, and is carried further. I could stay here a while—it is so homely and peaceful, but I feel a great urge to continue and reach my castle.

Gradually this beautiful landscape gives way to endless, monotonous fields. Industrial landscapes fill the far distance between me and the golden city of Prague. At lunchtime I find a nice spot under a young apple tree; but after this I dive into the greyness of urban landscapes.

First I come to the city of Melnik at the confluence of the rivers Elbe and Vltava. The city itself is perched high on a hill and you look down from there on the waterways and canals. I have tears in my eyes as I recall the long distance that I walked along such waterways in Belgium; and now there is a connection, through my walking, between western and eastern Europe! Melnik is a city from the time of Karl IV. Here he had this country's first vineyard planted, and then he gave the city into the safe-keeping of one of his wives. It is the city of a queen! The cathedral houses a crypt which serves as a resting place for thousands of skeletons—a strange site to behold. How many destinies congregate here in this small place?

After Melnik my footpath (European long-distance path) suddenly ends without any explanation! I feel very indignant, but there is nothing for it but to navigate without its now familiar signposts. My path leads through water meadows, and after the recent rains I find myself getting quite wet and my feet soaked again. Later on, the path runs along the river, more or less, through young oak woods with lovely summer flowers, dog roses and elders. I visit Dvořák's birthplace in Nelahozeves and finally arrive in Kralupy.

This is a most ugly place, just 50 years old, roughly the same age as I! It was built to house the workers of the huge chemical factory. The whole town consists of nothing but blocks of flats and has no discernible centre. My host family shows me round on bicycles. For them it is home; they have lived here all their lives. Tomorrow I will be in Prague! I can hardly believe it.

The next day it is pouring with rain. I reluctantly decide to hold off and have a rest day. I telephone Karel Dolista, the man I want to meet in Prague, who has worked as a guide to the Karlstein Castle in the past and holds a store of knowledge. He is also looking forward to meeting me, so I am overjoyed.

The next morning it is still raining, but I am not letting this stop me any longer! Around midday the sun comes out but I am so completely soaked through that I have to go behind some bushes and change. The path is along the Vltava all the way now until I reach the suburb of Suchdol, where my friends Eva and Pavel live with their two children. We meet full of joy and excitement! I remember writing to Pavel about my idea of doing this and he had replied: 'What a mad idea, but I love it!'

Now Pavel offers to accompany me on the last stretch into Prague. It is 12 June and the first sunny day in a very long time. Pavel, his dog and I start out together and Pavel takes me to a rocky outcrop from where you can see the city of Prague in all its glory. From here he explains to me the general layout and the characteristics of the different surrounding suburbs. Then we descend into one of those suburbs and walk through the famous park of Ledna to the river. Now at last we reach the beautiful Charles Bridge built in honour of Karl IV. I feel like a queen entering *her* city in a festival procession as I walk over this bridge, with Pavel at my side, and there is no end to my utter joy and elation! *I have arrived!* And I have walked all the way, on foot, and therefore this city belongs to me! She is mine and will always be! I want to hug everybody to share my joy, but I restrain myself and only Pavel has to endure such treatment. He is so happy for me! The golden city greets me in her best garment, shining in sunlight. I bathe in this true highlight of my life.

In the afternoon I meet up with Karel Dolista. I had pictured him as an old, wise man with white hair and a beard, filled with knowledge and wisdom. Instead I see a very lively, youthful man in his early forties, quite small in stature, with lively eyes and a friendly manner. He invites me for dinner and tells me the legend of St Wenceslas. Though the last of the Grail Kings, he only found this out at the moment of his violent death at the hands of his brother.

My soul is full to the brim. I go to the chapel of St Wenceslas in the cathedral and give thanks for this moment in my life.

The following days are spent in inner and outer preparations for the last leg of the journey, to the Karlstein Castle. I meet a few more times with Karel, who instructs me further in the historical origins of the Czech people and the life of Karl IV. He also introduces me to his potter friend, Michal, who is a keen walker himself and knows the paths to the castle very well. He recommends a particular route, and says to be sure to arrive early enough in the day to leave time to spend in the castle. He suggests that I split the walk into two days, passing a night in Trebonice, which is the very place where the queen used to rest on her journey from Prague to the castle. One can still see there a beautiful Romanesque chapel, which I could visit.

Michal is an artist as well as a potter. He has wild ginger hair and wants desperately to tell me lots of things, but his

English is quite poor and we have to rely on translation. He works with semi-precious stones that he melts and incorporates into his pottery. He is also an alchemist, engaged in the transformation of substance as mirror of soul transformation.

It is these three friends and spiritual brothers, Pavel, Karel and Michal (Paul, Charles, Michael), who together enable me to walk this last stretch. All three are important and give me nourishment, encouragement and love on the way. I am indebted to them.

The Road to the Castle

It is Monday, 18 June when I leave Prague. The day does not start well for me. I am not prepared. For two long hours I get lost in the city's suburbs and cannot find my path. Finally I have to return to Suchdol to fetch the compass I had forgotten—I have lost a lot of time. When at last I am on the right track I notice a huge black cloud covering half the sky, announcing an imminent thunderstorm. I run for shelter to a bus stop and wait for the deluge to stop. I feel utterly desolate and alone.

Despite these mishaps I do manage to reach Trebonice before dark and am met by both Karel and Michal, who furnish me with final instructions for the important day tomorrow. In his pidgin English, Michal keeps saying: 'Promise me to take this particular path' (pointing it out on the map). 'It will not be signposted, but you have to promise me to take it! Promise! Promise!' I promise.

Tuesday 19 June is an unusually cold and windy day for the time of year. The footpath is tedious; it leads past large fields and through run-down villages. I feel small and unworthy and strangely depressed, and I cannot shake off these negative feelings. A strange sadness and anxiety accompanies me now. I cannot explain it even to myself. All the difficult inner experiences of my journey pass again through my soul. Will I be able to enter the castle? Will I be allowed to see its innermost sanctuaries for whose sake I have come all this way?

At this moment, in one particular spot, I recognize that I have been at this inner place in myself before, long ages ago; and though the feelings originate from the past, I realize they have accompanied me all my life. The castle has a far deeper meaning for me than I have so far discovered. It belongs profoundly to my destiny and my inner path. All the experiences of this pilgrimage belong to my deepest being, the difficult ones as well as the uplifting and sustaining ones, the sad and the joyful. They all fuse and melt into the moment now as I recognize the journey for what it is: the turning point in my soul where all that has been is moving through a tiny point of passage, and coming out on the other side as new recognition in the flame of my heart.

Now I come to the village of Kuchar, which Michal said was a gift which the emperor gave to his favourite cook in gratitude for his service. It is lunchtime and I have my midday bread under a linden tree. The dark cloud that enveloped my soul is now lifting, and within I experience the most brilliant sunshine, despite the still cloudy and cold weather. I have returned to my pilgrimage with the deepest joy in my heart, and recognition of the archetype of all such journeys as well as that of the castle, which cannot be far off now. I am also now able to accept whatever awaits me there and will not colour it with my expectations. It is right, after all, that I should approach my sacred goal in a different mood of soul to that of my entry into Prague, that I should come in humility as befits a pilgrim and receive what is offered, without demand.

With these thoughts I reach the crossroads of which Michal had spoken so insistently. The signpost does indeed point in a different direction to the one I have promised to take. I keep

my promise, of course, and the path immediately leads into a
dense wood that swallows me up. Despite tiny stirrings of
doubt I choose trust and confidence, and walk at a brisk pace,
not looking back, not stopping to check the map. And suddenly I find myself directly before the castle! I had not seen it
from a distance, as I had imagined I would all these many
weeks! I step onto the driveway leading up to the courtyard,
and I see the reason for my firm promise: the other path, the
official route, would have taken me past endless booths of
trinkets that line the road from the car park all the way up the
hill. I step into the courtyard and look at the castle for a long
time. Slowly I make my way to the ticket booth.

'I have a reservation.'

'We have expected you! You are very welcome!'

The woman in the booth comes out with a big bunch of
keys. She escorts me, alone, to the castle. First we go to the
chapel of Our Lady, which is filled with a group of tourists
listening to a guide talking. Here I find the frescoes of the
Apocalypse, chief among them the image of the woman
clothed with the sun, the stars above her head and the moon
under her feet. I also see a fresco with three depictions of Karl
IV: one as he receives a holy relic from the King of the East,
one as he receives a holy relic from the King of the West, and
the third showing how he places them into a golden cross.

Now we turn to the 'grave', which is really a narrow passage between the chapel of Our Lady and the chapel of St
Katherine. Here we are on our own; the groups are not led
through this narrow place. It is this chapel that served as the
emperor's personal meditation chamber, and where he
retreated into solitude between the days of Maundy Thursday
and Easter Sunday. The chapel walls are studded with semi-

precious stones edged with gold, including the ceiling, which has a large opal at its centre. In my studies I had come across a comment by Rudolf Steiner in which he spoke of precious stones providing an opportunity for supersensible beings to look into our inner soul. With this in mind, I can only imagine the magnitude of individuality of this emperor, who meditated in such a space, where he was surrounded by the 'sense organs' of those other beings, and exposed his soul to their gaze.

Last of all we enter the most sacred space of all, the chapel of the Holy Cross. I cannot begin to describe the impression on me as I stepped into this space. The chapel is proportioned in a way that makes one feel wholly perceived and met as a human being—it is big enough to embody the dignity of this place yet small enough to make one feel part of it. It is filled with wonderful paintings by Theoderich; the portraits of the people he painted seem alive with their personalities. Beneath the gallery of paintings, the walls are studded with semi-precious stones set in gold. The vaulted ceiling is fashioned of gold upon which are stencilled the shapes of sun and moon; and the stars are an array of pieces of transparent glass inlaid in the gold. Large gemstones hang from the ceiling, signifying the planets.

I bow my head and pray. I am filled with silent joy. Time stands still at this moment, space opens for me and I become aware of those people who have been formative to my life's journey, together with those who have been part of my pilgrimage, enabling me to be in this sacred space. I have arrived.

Postscript

As I celebrate the end of my pilgrimage, I want to give thanks to the many people who have, in one way or another, accompanied me and made it possible: my family and friends, my colleagues, and over a hundred hosts and people whom I met along the way. I also give thanks to those mentioned in this book who have died. They too contributed their gifts. And to the invisible beings of my path; and my special companion, Solitude, whom it has been a privilege to know, and who I know will call me in times to come so that we may walk together again.

But what happens at the end of such a journey?

Before starting my journey I had written to Satish Kumar, requesting a meeting. He kindly invited me to his office at Dartington College keenly interested in what I was about to do. He gave me several pieces of advice, some of a very practical nature, such as using pieces of sheep's wool found in the fields to treat blisters—although as it happened, setting off in the middle of winter, this was sadly unavailable to me! But in particular he said one thing that kept ringing in my ears: *The most difficult part of such a journey is to return!*

After arriving in Prague I spent a couple of weeks wandering about on my own, to get to know this wonderful city of mine. I also treated myself to a performance of Dvorak's opera *Rusalka* in Prague's splendid opera house.

When the time came for me to return home I decided to travel by coach since I could not bear the thought of flying—

it would simply have been too fast. Interestingly the coach journey to London took exactly 22 hours. This intrigued me, as I had been on the road for 22 weeks.

Even this was too fast however. I was now used to a walking pace and after the amazing experience of my pilgrimage, I felt like a lost soul at home—restless and uncertain. I needed to walk every day and yet I had important preparation to do—I was due to fly to Japan and give a course. This thought terrified me. How could I go to such a far-flung place, further away than I had ever been before, and encounter an entirely different culture?

One fine evening I took a walk with Rosemary's mother, wishing to hear about the last weeks and days of her life. I heard that up to her last day Rosemary retained her sense of humour, sitting up in bed and singing 'This will be the day that I die!' and being rebuked by her carer for being so frivolous! Ann, Rosemary's mother, is a very lively and fit old lady with boundless energy. Together we climbed a hill near my house to watch the magnificent sunset paint itself before our eyes. We were debating whether to return the same way or to walk through a woodland to make it a circular walk. We opted for the latter as we both knew the area so well that we were sure we could easily find our way in the dark.

By the time we reached the woodland, it was indeed pitch black. The path was quite uneven and sloped down steeply on one side with pathways made by busy badgers. I walked on ahead and frequently turned around to make sure that Ann was all right. We were nearly home when turning round once more, my right foot got caught in a root and I fell down the slope. As I did so I was convinced I heard a crack! Sure enough, when I tried to get up again the searing pain in my ankle was too much. Poor Ann had to fight her way through the last bit of woodland to fetch Bernard to the scene. He engineered a heroic rescue effort with some ropes to get me down the slope safely.

The next day I found that I had fractured my ankle. My trip to Japan was too close to undertake with my leg in plaster, so I had to find a colleague to run the course for me.

I soon realized that my invisible travelling companion had a hand in this incident! This was the only way to stop me from 'carrying on' the journey endlessly in my mind. Now I had to relinquish my cherished independence and allow myself to be completely cared for by my husband. He had to help me get washed and dressed, and carry me about from the house to the garden and back again, drive me to hospital appointments and soothe my spirits, all of which he accomplished beauti-fully. I enjoyed his company and endless patience, and the way he brought home little treats and surprises. I managed to wholly accept this situation as soon as I saw the wisdom of destiny. I used my enforced rest to study and do sketches in the garden and house. I also experienced, during a few out-ings, what it is like to be in a wheelchair. By the time term started I was able to walk on crutches and resume my teaching and therapy work.

There were many dark moments during this time. When I tried to start painting again I felt that I had lost any skill I ever had. I fell into deep despair, wondering whether I needed to renounce my art. After many fruitless starts I decided to work with the utmost simplicity, constricting my palette to three colours only, magenta, indigo and gold. Soon I was captivated by this unusual colour combination and found that they were perfectly suited to convey my experiences of the treasures of Karlstein Castle. Since then I have continued working with these colours and studied their significance, coming to the conclusion that, as a transformation of red, blue and yellow, they signify the alchemical transformation of the human soul.

When at last I dared include more colours again I was ready to explore the Foundation Stone Meditation through painting, the idea of which had already come to me during my journey. I created a set of seven paintings relating to the seven stanzas of the meditation, which have been printed as postcards. I have now met a number of people who told me that they are using these cards in their own study and meditation.

In other areas, too, I began to feel that 'the old clothes' no longer fitted and that I could not just carry on where I had left off. It took me a while to identify what it was that needed to change. Then there came a moment very clearly etched into my memory, just as I was waiting for an appointment outside in the sunshine, when I realized that I could no longer teach at Hibernia College, the place I had helped start ten years before. This was a most painful realization and yet I knew I would ignore the insight at my peril. It was a moment of utter clarity, and by now I had learned to listen.

Leaving Hibernia threw me into a renewed phase of restlessness, as I now only had two days' work each week as a therapist. I could feel another dark cloud approaching, threatening to envelop me. This moment coincided, however, with two of my children being in great need of support, and I was very grateful to have the time to offer it. Then my middle daughter announced that she was pregnant (a complete surprise to all of us and to herself). What a joy to hear this news, and what a privilege to be able to accompany her very closely on this journey which culminated in the birth of our little granddaughter Saskia in our house, with both Bernard and myself present at the birth!

Around this time, Melanie—who had been my host in Canterbury—decided to move to Stourbridge, an hour's journey away. We both remembered our wish to work together eventually. This seemed more possible now than ever before. One afternoon I came to visit her in her flat, and asked her whether she could see herself helping me start a support group for patients at St Luke's Medical Practice. I knew that Melanie had run a group like this at Blackthorn Medical Centre in Maidstone when she still lived in Canterbury. The new ingredient in my proposal was to combine counselling skills with art so that participants could have an immediate artistic experience of the processes they were undergoing. Developing new exercises in a social context with seriously ill people would be a growing point for me and would be a totally new departure for both of us. To my great joy Melanie agreed to my proposal, and we set to work straight away to plan this new venture.

We decided to adopt the name 'Oasis', the same that was used at Blackthorn, to honour the origin of this work and to supplement it with our different approach. At Easter 2003 we launched the Oasis work at St Luke's, and also opened it to patients not registered with the practice. The response was tremendous: we had to form two groups straight away and put people on a waiting list. We were fortunate to secure some funding from the 'Lottery Awards for All' and some anthroposophical trusts as well as individual donations. Two years later the trust set up by my late teacher, Vera Taberner —the Association for the Promotion of Artistic Therapy—

took us under its wings. This, more than anything else, felt like powerful confirmation of this impulse.

The Oasis work is still going strong in Stroud, even though Melanie is no longer able to travel there due to her own health issues. She has started a third Oasis group at Park Attwood Clinic and we have run a number of workshops together to help other people start similar groups, even travelling abroad to two locations in Spain. I am fortunate to have found a new colleague to continue the work with me in Stroud.

I soon realized that my main qualification for running such groups came from my pilgrimage to Karlstein Castle. The gift I received is a unique understanding of the profound meaning of journeying and how it can heal the wounds that hold us back. Many Oasis participants have come to the end of a particular road, with no signposts or compass for a new direction. We deliberately did not want to specialize on any particular illness. It so happened however that we attracted a good number of people with mental health problems who had been told they would require medication for the rest of their lives. This verdict was a huge wake-up call for some, and prompted them to seek another solution elsewhere. We see the Oasis work as support with a spiritual dimension. We try to make this experiential by focusing on biography as the spiritual signature of each individual. We are deeply moved by how this approach works in a most immediate and direct way and enables people to access their own source of health. We feel privileged to witness this process!

As for my personal life, the act of walking as a means to enter meditation is now firmly established. Every morning, from Monday to Friday, I rise at 6 o'clock and climb a near-by hill from which I can view the morning sky. During my ascent I inwardly go through a sequence of meditations, which includes acknowledging people close to me who have died and I reflect on the significance they have had in my life. When I arrive at the top I let go of all thoughts and take in the particular mood of that morning, celebrating it and giving thanks for another day.

I have found this practice to be of tremendous value and a source of inspiration. Whatever else happens in the day, I have this positive beginning! I walk whatever the weather, and have enjoyed wind, rain and storms, perfectly clear calm mornings or leaden grey heavy skies. Each mood communicates with me at a deep level. The experience of subtle changes through the seasons is greatly enhanced by noticing the rhythm of the light over the course of a year. This helps me sense how the earth organism itself has inbreath and outbreath. My daily walk is an invaluable source of inspiration, creating optimism for the day ahead. Most weekends I also find time for a whole-day walk in nature; and for a long-distance walk during the holidays.

My pilgrimage has its own special place in my biography. Inwardly, I divide my life into 'before' and 'after'. I feel that a deep and lasting change occurred because I was allowed to touch the horizon, and even to catch a glimpse of the pot of gold at the end of the rainbow!

After nearly seven years, the experience of my journey is as present for me now as if it happened yesterday. Whenever I feel the need to enter into the experience I just call up one of the images from it and find myself walking along again with my invisible companion.

I mentioned my dear maternal grandmother at the beginning of this account. Now, at the end, I must close this story with the wonderful privilege of being a grandmother myself, and storyteller to my own little grandchild Saskia, with the task of instilling in her images that will give her courage and conviction, spiritual certainty and trust in destiny.

October 2007

Foundation Stone Meditation

Rudolf Steiner

Human Soul!
You live in the limbs
Which bear you through the world of space
Within the flowing ocean of the spirit:
Practise *spirit re-cognition*
In depths of soul,
Where in the wielding will
Of world creating
The individual I
Comes to being
In the I of God;
And you will truly *live*
In your body's cosmic being.

For the Father Spirit of the heights is present
In world depths begetting existence:
Spirits of Strength!
May there ring forth from the heights
The call re-echoed in the depths;
Proclaiming:
Humankind is born of God.
The elemental spirits hear it
In east, west, north, south:
*May hu*man beings *hear it!*

Human Soul!
You live in the beat of heart and lung

Which leads you through the rhythm of time
Into the realm of your own soul's feeling.
Practise *spirit presence*
In soul composure,
Where the weaving deeds
Of universal becoming
Unite
The individual I
With the I of the World;
And you will truly *feel*
In the active life of your soul.

For the Christ Will is present all around
In world rhythms shedding grace on our souls;
Spirits of Light!
May what is formed by the west
Have been quickened in the light of the east;
Proclaiming:
In Christ death becomes life.
The elemental spirits hear it
In east, west, north, south:
May human beings hear it!

Human Soul!
You live in the stillness of the head
Which from the founts of eternity
Discloses for you cosmic thoughts:
Practise *spirit beholding*
In thought calm,
Where the eternal aims of Gods
Give the light of spirit worlds

To the individual I
For will in freedom.
And you will truly *think*
In the founts of your human spirit.

For the Spirit's cosmic thoughts are present
In world existence begging for light;
Spirits of Soul!
May there ascend from the depths
The plea heard in the heights;
Proclaiming:
In the Spirit's cosmic thoughts the soul will awaken.
The elemental spirits hear it
In east, west, north, south:
*May hu*man beings *hear it!*

At the turning of time
Cosmic Spirit Light descended
Into the earthly stream of being;
Darkness of night
Had run its course;
The light of day
Shone forth in human souls:
Light
That gives warmth
To poor shepherds' hearts,
Light
That enlightens
The wise heads of kings.

God-given light,
Christ Sun

Give warmth
To our hearts;
Give light
To our heads;
That what we found
From our hearts
What we guide
From our heads
Will be good.

Translation: Pauline Wehrle
From: *The Foundation Stone Meditation*, Rudolf Steiner Press, 2005.

Notes

1. In the Old Testament story, Tobit, to find a cure for his blindness, sends his son on a journey, and advises him to go to the marketplace.

2. Biodynamic agriculture was originally inspired by a series of eight lectures given by Rudolf Steiner in 1924, making it the oldest consciously organic form of agriculture. It is an approach that takes account of the spiritual as well as the material processes of life and is one of the most sustainable forms of agriculture in existence. It is now a worldwide movement spanning five continents. For more information contact: Biodynamic Agricultural Association, Painswick Inn Project, Gloucester Street, Stroud GL5 1HF. *www.biodynamic.org.uk*.

   The Three Kings' Preparation is widely used on biodynamic farms. It differs from the other biodynamic preparations in that it does not directly stimulate soil vitality but is, rather, a blessing for the earth and all her unseen helpers in the elemental world. It was developed by Hugo Erbe, an early biodynamic farmer. He experienced how the earth was deeply wounded when the atom bomb was dropped on Hiroshima. Even on his own farm in Central Europe great confusion was caused within the elemental world and he felt that powerfully harmful forces were unleashed. It was to counteract this and re-establish harmony that Hugo Erbe developed a preparation made from gold, frankincense and myrrh, three sacred treasures of the ancient orient.

3. A New Year's Eve tradition, in which lead is melted over a fire then cast into cold water. The shapes produced can be used to predict events of the coming year.

4. Henry Hoth & Co., 1997.

5. Peter Mortimer, *Broke through Britain—One Man's Penniless Odyssey*, Mainstream Publ., 1999.

6. Jean Vanier started the first L'Arche Community in France in 1964. It is now an international organization providing family-like homes and care for adults with special needs.

7. Two years after my return, Melanie moved to Stourbridge, West Midlands. We met up again and together started a support group for people with chronic health problems, called Oasis, at St Luke's Medical Centre in Stroud, Gloucester-shire. See further in Postscript.

8. The Foundation Stone Meditation was given by Rudolf Steiner at the founding of the General Anthroposophical Society at the Goetheanum in Dornach, Switzerland, during the Christmas Holy Nights of 1923–4. Just as a physical building can be given a foundation stone so too can a society—a society is after all an organized structure too. Anthroposophical Societies exist in many countries throughout the world. Each one is also part of the worldwide General Anthroposophical Society. Its purpose is to cultivate understanding for the pioneering research undertaken by Rudolf Steiner, to encourage individuals of all countries, religions and ethnic backgrounds to celebrate their common humanity and pursue their unique individual journeys.

9. Advent, Christmas, Epiphany are festivals connected with the Father God, and each in turn is related to the Trinity in the following way:

Advent—Father
Christmas—Son
Epiphany—Holy Spirit

Lent, Easter, Ascension are festivals of the Son-God and sub-divided thus:

Lent—Father
Easter—Son
Ascension—Holy Spirit

Whitsun, St John's, Michaelmas are connected with the mystery of the Holy Spirit and each in turn belongs like this:

Whitsun—Father
St John's—Son
Michaelmas—Spirit

10. One of the descendants of Cain who first forged brass and other metals.

11. Walter Ulbricht was the President of the German Democratic Republic from 1950 to 1971 and first secretary of Socialist Unity (Communist) Party. He played a key role in the early development of East Germany.

12. Erich Honecker took over from Ulbricht in 1971 and presided until shortly before the collapse of the Communist regime.